# Management for Professionals

The Springer series "Management for Professionals" comprises high-level business and management books for executives, MBA students, and practice-oriented business researchers. The topics cover all themes relevant to businesses and the business ecosystem. The authors are experienced business professionals and renowned professors who combine scientific backgrounds, best practices, and entrepreneurial vision to provide powerful insights into achieving business excellence.

The Series is SCOPUS-indexed.

C.-Andreas Dalluege • John Stephen Gary Wells
Editors

# Navigating an EU Research Project

## Managing Challenges to Deliver Success

Springer

*Editors*
C.-Andreas Dalluege
IBK (Germany)
Wiesbaden, Hessen, Germany

John Stephen Gary Wells
School of Health Sciences
South East Technological University
Waterford, Ireland

ISSN 2192-8096 ISSN 2192-810X (electronic)
Management for Professionals
ISBN 978-3-031-70930-2 ISBN 978-3-031-70928-9 (eBook)
https://doi.org/10.1007/978-3-031-70928-9

This work was supported by Erasmus+



This Springer imprint is published by the registered company Springer Nature Switzerland AG
The registered company address is: Gewerbestrasse 11, 6330 Cham, Switzerland

# Foreword

I am delighted to contribute a foreword for Navigating an EU Research Project, edited by Dalluege and my colleague John Wells.

Immersing oneself in research to generate new knowledge is simultaneously a wonderful privilege and a responsibility. Part of that responsibility is to foster collaborations and partnerships towards a common goal. EU Research projects, in particular, engender such networking. Striving with other researchers across Europe to tackle a shared problem relies on building relationships across European jurisdictions and that is also the privilege of engaging in research. Strong research collaboration frequently comes from, or leads to, interpersonal professional relationships that are both fruitful and enduring.

No laboratory is an island (to channel the poet John Donne) and research findings rarely spring into existence without antecedents or collaborative encounters. A vibrant pan-European project partnership facilitates synergy of diverse laboratories. The productivity gains from such an enterprise should not be underestimated.

Of course, research and collaboration demand financial support and we are fortunate to have access to various funding schemes provided by the EU. Ireland is one country that has benefitted greatly from access to European funding in recent decades and has built considerable expertise in, and knowledge of, the application, management, and reporting structures associated with EU research projects.

In this timely book the contributors have generously shared their craft, experiences, and successes of EU research funding procurement. It forms a practical guide to the novice researcher as they navigate this funding stream. The book offers clear, sensible, and pragmatic advice from the initial phase of establishing networks, through grant application to implementation, management, budgets, and reporting. It is recognised that the EU application process and templates can be complex and bureaucratic. The brilliance of this book is that it completely demystifies the process! Each section outlines key steps: what the reviewers are likely to expect, how to maximise the strength of the application and how to articulate impact. The importance of building and maintaining relationships, as well as leveraging the combined expertise of the network is reinforced throughout.

While this book draws much from the experience of the authors in health-related EU projects such as DDS-MAP, ROSE, and SSTeMM, it is an excellent tool to assist researchers from any discipline in support of their engagement with EU projects. I have no doubt that this book will be used widely by the researcher community and those from university Research Offices who support the application process.

EU funding is important and continues to have impact on the European research ecosystem. Navigating an EU Research Project should encourage and assist those wishing to engage with EU funding calls and the authors have given great service to researchers in compiling this authoritative handbook towards EU research project success.

South East Technological University (SETU) Veronica Campbell
Waterford, Ireland

# Foreword

In public discourse the benefits of European Union membership are often questioned, and the speed and efficiency of EU processes are frequently criticised. However, one often-cited area and example of successful European integration are EU-funded research programmes. Internationally, European research funding is considered a role model for multilateral cooperation and collaboration. The benefits and synergies of EU projects go far beyond their specific research objectives and allow for an intense intellectual and cultural exchange and a successful manifestation of the pan-European idea. For this reason, I personally found EU projects most interesting and rewarding!

However, EU research projects are far from easy to get, to properly administer and manage, and, to successfully complete! The funding landscape is broad, the requirements for each funding scheme are highly specific and the accompanying manuals are not exactly entertaining reading material. The probability of a proposal's success is typically low and even in the event of a successful proposal there are administrative and legal hurdles to overcome before a project can even be started. Finally, there is the challenge of putting the project plan that was "dreamed up" into practise and delivering the promised results, while keeping the project partners committed to the common objective.

While browsing through this book, the first thought that came to my mind was: "Why has it not been written before?". I personally would have benefitted tremendously from the collected experience of the authors, although some of that knowledge has transpired through the proposals and projects we did together and some of the techniques and examples looked pleasingly familiar. Nevertheless, this compilation of many person-years of experience in EU funding and acquisition and management of EU projects will be helpful for newcomers and seasoned EU-project veterans alike. The content is delivered in a very natural cadence of how such projects are acquired, started and delivered and the practical illustrations will most certainly raise the probability of success of such endeavours.

Good luck and many ground-breaking EU projects to all of us!

FH Wien der Wirtschaftkammer Wien — Walter Mayrhofer
Wien, Austria

# Contents

# Chapter 1
# Introduction: What This Book Is About and Why We Wrote It

**C.-Andreas Dalluege and John Stephen Gary Wells**

The idea for this book came about when one of our EU-funded projects—SSTeMM (Student Stress Training e-Mobile Management—https://sstemm.eu/) was confronted with the 'lockdown' challenges of the Covid Pandemic between 2020 and 2021. Our target group—student nurses and their clinical mentors—were suddenly diverted to urgent duties outside of their normal education and training experience and became, as a result, inaccessible to the project team for a considerable length of time.

In addition, many of the SSTeMM team itself were drawn from higher education and clinical services and faced in their day-to-day work challenges outside of the project arising from 'the lockdown'. Yet the project outcomes, in terms of contractual obligations with the EU, still had to be met. Once having met these challenges successfully, the project team came together to reflect on their learning from what had been, at times, a very stressful experience for all involved.

Arising from these discussions it was decided that other current and future researchers might benefit from our experience of dealing with project management and implementation challenges, not just in relation to SSTeMM during the COVID lockdown, but also our accumulated experience of managing over 50 European Union- funded projects successfully and in the case of some authors having evaluated over 100 EU-funding proposals.

This book therefore addresses the often daunting and stressful nature of applying for EU research funding. It provides guidance, based on our experience, about what

C.-A. Dalluege
IBK, Wiesbaden, Germany
e-mail: cad@ibk.eu

J. S. G. Wells (✉)
South East Technological University, Waterford, Ireland
e-mail: john.wells@setu.ie



C.-A. Dalluege, J. S. G. Wells (eds.), *Navigating an EU Research Project*, Management for Professionals, https://doi.org/10.1007/978-3-031-70928-9_1

you need to consider when writing and submitting a 'winning' proposal. It also provides advice on how to manage a funded project to its successful conclusion.

By sharing our experiences and lessons from a range of projects, we hope to provide practical insights, advice, and guidance for applicants and researchers, particularly for those new to the experience of applying for EU funding and managing a funded project so that outcomes are successful for you, the reader.

We describe when and how we received support from the EU to reduce the stress and burden on us during the pandemic. Through this description, we aim to highlight why such support should become standard practice by EU research and project funding agencies for applicants and researchers. This will ensure that practice within these agencies aligns with the Commission's policy priorities for improving mental health and well-being within the workforce and the broader population of the European Union.

This book, therefore, is designed to help you, the reader, understand:

- How to navigate the often complex application process in relation to European Union project calls with a focus on Erasmus and Horizon calls (though the general principles outlined within the narrative can be applied to most nationally funded project calls).
- How to select a programme or call that fits with your own research idea.
- How to use a strategic approach to select a consortium composition that will maximise your chances of winning funding and successfully complete a project.
- How to interlink previously funded research projects carried out by consortium partners into your current application.

We also aim to:

- Provide real-world experience of managing and implementing EU-funded projects to a successful conclusion despite unexpected challenges.
- Highlight the importance of building relationships with EU funding agencies and explore the challenges of engaging with such agencies during the submission process and following a successful outcome.
- Provide advice on how to write a successful report at the end of the project timeline.

We hope this book will equip the reader with the tools, knowledge, and confidence needed successfully to navigate the EU submission process and thereby secure project funding. By sharing our insights and experiences, we want to contribute to a more supportive and transparent funding landscape that benefits both researchers and the broader European community.

## 1.1 Emphasising a 'Real-World' Approach to Promote Well-Being

Applying for and participating in multinational funded research projects has become an important part of a successful academic career in higher education, as well as for research-oriented commercial organisations. Such participation profiles experience in working with multi-disciplinary research-oriented teams, networking across national and international partnerships, demonstrate the acquisition and production of new knowledge and show the ability to win third-party funding for one's own institution.

Within Europe, the largest funder of such research is the European Commission principally through the Horizon and Erasmus funding schemes and other associated programmes. Therefore, to progress a research-oriented career it is important to win funding or participate in a funded project from this source.

Despite the availability of various resources and guides, many applicants and researchers still struggle with navigating the complexities of building partnerships, the submission process and ensuring the successful implementation of their projects should funding be won. The stress and pressure associated with the process of applying for funding and, if successful, managing a funded project can take a significant toll on the individual and a team's well-being, potentially compromising their work quality.

This book, by sharing practical experiences and discussing how challenges, both foreseen and unforeseen, can be mitigated, aims to contribute to a more holistic understanding of the EU application for funding and project implementation process. It is for this reason that this book's emphasises a 'real-world' approach and reflection.

Through our reflective approach, we want to underscore that application and administrative processes in relation to major funding calls need to implement EU policy priorities with regard to the promotion of mental health and well-being for all those that engage with application procedures, including those within the EU who administer the application and project oversight process. Through emphasising our 'real-world' experience we want this book to promote a healthier, more supportive environment for all those involved in research funding—that is, researchers, outside stakeholders, and those employed within the funding agencies. We will have more to say on this in the final chapter.

In relation to the above, the importance of building strong relationships with EU funding agencies (and by this we mean getting to know the personnel in the agencies and communicating with them) will foster effective partnerships to maximise the chances of success in terms of project outcomes and people's well-being. We have found the better the relationship, the more supportive the agency is in terms of advice giving and negotiating. These aspects are often underrepresented in existing literature, yet they play a crucial role in both a positive experience and a successful outcome of EU-funded projects.

In summary, we think this book is valuable for anyone involved in EU-funded projects or considering applying for such funding. It offers practical insights, expert advice, and real-world examples to help readers navigate the complexities of the process, foster effective partnerships, and address the often-overlooked challenges related to mental health and well-being. Through these insights, we hope to contribute to a more transparent, accessible, and supportive funding landscape for researchers and applicants across Europe.

## 1.2 How the Book Is Structured

This book is not the usual 'academic' book with lots of references (we do have a few, but not many). This book content is structured entirely through our experiences of working on many EU-funded projects. We have held diverse project roles such as principal investigators/project co-ordinators, senior researchers, EU project evaluators, and project administrators. This book therefore is structured through our personal experiences of success and what we have learned as a result. To illustrate key points, we use examples from our recently completed SSTeMM project and sometimes from other projects in which we have been involved (a list of some of these can be found in Appendix B) to provide 'real-world' context and hopefully make it easier for you to understand some points we want to make.

The content is organised into chapters, each focusing on a specific aspect of the project lifecycle. This approach ensures that readers can easily follow the process from beginning to end, gaining valuable insights and practical advice along the way. You should note, however, that the complexities involved in applying for funding and managing a project do not neatly fit into self-contained boxes. Inevitably, there will be crossovers between chapters. When this occurs, we will draw readers' attention to these by referring to chapters where similar information is mentioned.

Throughout the book, we emphasise the importance of clear communication, collaboration, and strategic thinking in every aspect of project planning and implementation. To facilitate understanding and engagement, we present the information in a reader-friendly format, incorporating various visual aids, such as charts, tables, and diagrams, to clarify concepts and present data in an accessible manner.

We also provide you with practical tips, checklists, and, in Appendix C, a link to templates to help you to apply the lessons we have learned to your projects. These resources aim to support you whilst developing your proposal, building partnerships, and managing your project effectively.

In addition to the main content, the book includes, in its appendices, supplementary materials, such as a list of EU programmes available at the time of writing this book, a list and description of some of the projects we have either led or partnered within a consortium, a bibliography of publications which we think you might find useful, and a link to templates that you can use for your own project.

## 1.3 What Is a Funding Call?

Throughout this book, we focus on how to apply for a grant in response to an EU-funding call. The EU runs a wide range of research-oriented programmes and allocates one of the most significant budgets to fund research-related programmes in the world (a list of current funding programmes (i.e. Summer 2024) can be found in Appendix A).

Whilst EU funding comes in many different forms, the most common is a grant. Typically, people apply for grants by submitting ideas for projects following a call for proposals. For example, the HORIZON programme has an allocated budget of €95.5 billion for 2021–2027. Under identified themes for this budget allocation, Horizon each year issues specific calls for researchers to submit applications to fund proposals that are aligned with the specific call. This approach is replicated by the different programmes run by the EU, for example ERASMUS+.

Most of the experience that the editors and contributors to this book have had has been in relation to applying for grants. Thus, we focus mostly on content as this relates to calls issued by Erasmus Plus, Horizon, and EU4Health programmes—and their prior iterations, such as Leonardo de Vinci.

## 1.4 Conclusion

Overall, this book will provide you with a comprehensive guide to the EU-funded project process, enriched by our real-world experiences and insights. We want to empower you with the confidence to navigate the complexities of the formulation, application, and management process of a project successfully.

**C.-Andreas Dalluege** Founder and Managing Partner of IBK Group; Chairman of the European Business Excellence Network e.V.; National Council Member of the Irish Work Study Institute. Certified Advisor & Trainer of EFQM, Operating Partner and Trainer of Initiative Ludwig-Erhard-Preis (ILEP).

Since 1990 he participated as the senior researcher for his organisation in over 35 EU projects in most programme types offered by the EU and represented his company in all of them at the Management Board level as well as worked as our lead researcher in them.

He serves on the national board of the Irish Work Study Institute (IIESMS) and as President of the European Business Excellence Network (EuroBEN).

As a lecturer at the TH Aschaffenburg, he also gives classes on the design, proposing, and running of EU Research projects since 2019. Contact: cad@ibk.eu

**John Stephen Gary Wells** PhD, FAAN, FNMFRCSI (Ad Eundem) is Dean of the School of Health Sciences at the South East Technological University. John graduated from the University of Manchester with a degree in history. Following graduation, he trained and practised as a mental health nurse in London, eventually managing one of the busiest acute psychiatric admission units in the capital. John then transitioned from a clinical practice role to an academic one in 1993, moving to Ireland in 1998 to take up an academic position there.

John is an active and experienced researcher. As either Principal Investigator or co-investigator he has won funding from national and EU-funded research programmes to the value of 12 million Euros. He is a member of the National Research Ethics Committee for Clinical Trials in Ireland and holds visiting professorships at UCD, Ireland, King's College London, UK, and Maribor University, Slovenia. John has published 115 peer-reviewed papers, 7 technical reports (commissioned by regional, national, and EU agencies), 9 book chapters and 1 book.

At the time of publication he is principal investigator for an EU4Health-funded project on enhancing the digital skills of the pan-European health care workforce. He is also chairperson of a COST Action on expanding the access of people with intellectual disabilities to cancer services. Contact: john.wells@setu.ie

# Chapter 2
# Preparing to Make an EU Application

**C.-Andreas Dalluege, Dominika Vrbnjak, Majda Pajnkihar, and John Stephen Gary Wells**

This chapter describes some key activities in which you need to engage in preparation to make an application in response to an EU funding Call. The very foundation of an application is the strength of your relationship with partners in the proposed consortium within an application. We therefore start with approaches on how to build these. This is a long-term activity that takes time but pays dividends when it comes to quickly establishing a consortium when a Call issued.

We describe key activities you should engage in to identify the right funding call to suit your field of interest/ project idea. The earlier you start this, the better. Once identified familiarisation with the detail will pay dividends when writing your application, so we describe how you should do this.

## 2.1 Building Relationships Over Time

Building a consortium from 'scratch' in response to a Call for applications for proposal funding can be a significant stressor when preparing and writing a proposal. Therefore, it is important that over time you establish friendships, relationships, and contacts with significant others in your field of interest across the EU. A shared

C.-A. Dalluege (✉)
IBK, Wiesbaden, Germany
e-mail: cad@ibk.eu

D. Vrbnjak · M. Pajnkihar
University Maribor, Maribor, Slovenia
e-mail: dominika.vrbnjak@um.si; majda.pajnkihar@um.si

J. S. G. Wells
South East Technological University, Waterford, Ireland
e-mail: john.wells@setu.ie



C.-A. Dalluege, J. S. G. Wells (eds.), *Navigating an EU Research Project*, Management for Professionals, https://doi.org/10.1007/978-3-031-70928-9_2

history and trust built over time can provide support and expertise often benefits a project in terms of open communication, a reduction in conflict, and a shared understanding of goals. In addition, such relationships greatly facilitate both speed of response to a Call and reduce the stress involved when preparing and writing your application.

Relationship building, therefore, with other individuals who share your research interests is a crucial part of project advancement. Building such relationships involves an element of serendipity such as fortuitous encounters with individuals both within your own country and abroad. It is an endeavour that requires effort on your part and a commitment to authenticity in which you will support others when called upon. So, the rhetorical question is how do 'I' do this? Based on our own experiences below is what we have learned.

It is important when building such connections that they are rooted in mutual positive regard (that is you like each other!), friendliness, and sustained contact. If they are purely transactional in nature, they are less likely to be maintained over time. That is not to say that a transactional relationship cannot develop into a trusting friendship; it is just that we have found they are harder to maintain.

We see sustained contact and friendship between individuals as a key element of success in developing an application. It is easier to work with people you have gotten to know over time than working with people who you do not know.

To build such trusting and mutually positive relationships project a persona of being approachable to people and genuinely interested in them. If you show interest in others, then generally most people will also be interested in you and will want to stay in contact.

Another approach to relationship building is to seek recommendations from contacts you already have about people who might be interested in a project you are planning. Referrals from trusted sources can often lead to long-term fruitful partnerships. For example, this is how the two editors of this book (Wells in Ireland and Dalluege in Germany) first met nine years ago and have become friends and successfully collaborated on a range of projects since.

If working from a 'cold' starting point, i.e. not having such relationships, then attend networking events, conferences, and workshops to establish connections, with individuals with cognate interests. Actively contact those recommended to you by your collegial friends at work. It is also worth attending national briefings (if possible, in person) on EU funding calls. These are often held by the relevant EU agency in your country and when held in person are an excellent networking opportunity.

Additionally consider joining communities such as forums, social media groups, and professional networks. These platforms provide opportunities to connect with professionals and organisations who share interests. They also offer a space for idea exchange. Keep up-to-date with the developments in your field.

An excellent example of a professional network/group with which many of us (the writers of this book) are involved is the Udine C Network—Understanding Development Issues, in Nurse Educator Careers. This group aims to promote friendship, respect, and intellectual exchange among healthcare professionals in nursing research, education, and practice development across member countries. We have developed friendships and partnerships within this group, which have subsequently greatly facilitated a series of successful proposal developments between members who are friends as well as colleagues.

On first encounters, do not forget to exchange contact information whether it is through business cards or digital alternatives like LinkedIn, email, or WhatsApp. Always follow up on an initial meeting by sending a message expressing your gratitude for the meeting and reiterate your interest in collaborating or staying in touch. Such contact will facilitate these relationships to become familial so that when the time comes you can call upon them to join an application for a specific call.

As a means of establishing friendships, it is worth working with partners on small initiatives to establish working relationships. For example, look at established programmes such as those funded by the COST initiative and join these for networking and relationship building opportunities.

## 2.2 The Value of Liaising with the National Contact Point (NCP)

Aligning your project idea with the chosen funding call is essential. You may need objective assessment of the alignment of your idea and the experience and capacity of your team with a specific funding call. Your National Contact Point (NCP) can be very useful for this purpose, as they know the grant calls intimately and are often privy to non-public information and other contexts that can affect the success of your application. We suggest you develop a 'bond' relationship with your NCPs by seeking their counsel in advance of a projected Call to which you intend to apply to make them aware of your intention to apply and speak to them regularly as you go through the process of application.

Your NCP can act as a sounding board for your proposal. They may have practical tips (for example, dealing with issues around the portal platform) and may be able to point you to areas or documents to consider (for example, EU Pact for Skills). In some cases, they may give practical tips and suggestions around specific elements of your application.

Other benefits when contacting with your NCP include:

- **Unique expertise**: NCPs are likely to have an intimate understanding of the chosen Call's eco-system including the portal, general submission processes, priority areas, and important aspects to consider.
- **Well-informed about explicit requirements**: NCPs are likely to be well-informed about all requirements associated with Calls ranging from geographic profile of participants across Europe (for certain Calls beyond Europe), discipline requirements, and adherence to open science principles. In the case of the latter, open science is now often an expectation within applications for EU Calls.

- **Well-informed about implicit requirements**: NCPs are likely to have attended specific briefings by the responsible programme officers in Brussels (where the EU-funded programmes are head quartered) in advance of the issuing of a Call. As a result, they may have added context that enables them to suggest elements that you need to highlight in your application that may not be so obvious in the text of the Call when issued.
- **Networked**: NCPs have exposure to a wide range of consortia. They may be able to suggest potential partners and/or suggest useful perspectives to include (for example, including Small and Medium Enterprise—SMEs—partners).
- **Up-to-date information**: Sometimes information changes, even after a Call is issued. NCPs can keep you updated about such changes if you ask them to do so.
- **Administrative support**: Once funded, NCPs can also provide invaluable support in the provision of advice for the next steps in relation to administrative expectations.

In summary, NCPs are valuable resources to identify and utilise at all stages of your grant application. It is advisable to identify and contact your grant call NCP as soon as possible as they can be helpful throughout the process from planning, preparation to execution.

## 2.3 Identifying the Right Funding Call

A strategic approach to proposal/project planning is to start it well in advance of any specific programme Call. Do not limit yourself to one identified Call. You should also explore avenues that can create synergies with your research ideas in other programme Calls. For instance, if you have a fundable concept for a Horizon Research and Innovation project consider whether there are different programme Calls in cognate areas that would allow you to extend your research proposal topic towards these Calls. Investigate such programmes as ERASMUS Plus Partnership building Calls that can help develop materials and connections that would support your proposal for more ambitious future funding under Horizon.

There are many funding calls issued by the EU over the course of any one year by these EU programmes. For example, under Horizon there are many Programme strands. Within these programmes they have themes from which they then develop specific calls. Usually, the Programme will indicate in advance (usually the prior year) when these calls are likely to happen and what they will cover. The result is you might see more than one call that may be relevant to your proposed project.

To maximise your chances of securing EU funding it is therefore crucial to identify the right funding Call that most closely aligns with your project idea. This entails aligning your project's objectives, scope, and target audience with a call that matches your potential consortium's expertise and available resources.

To do this, you need to prepare your general concepts within an area of focus so that when a Call is issued these can be adapted to the requirements of a specific programme. In thinking about this, you should consider the following questions to develop a set of answers/rationale that can be later deployed within a specific proposal:

- Do you aim to develop and test an entirely new concept or intervention?
- Do you want to take an existing concept and refine it into a commercially viable solution? (one should remember in this regard that the EU has strict conditions in relation to using research funding to develop a commercial outcome with its default position being that anything developed using EU funding should be open access).
- Is your goal to explore markets?
- Do you intend to expand your network by engaging with knowledge fields or geographical areas that are not specifically represented within your consortium?

Answering this type of question will help you identify potential Calls with which you can align your broad proposal idea into a specific proposal. In this regard, here are some steps you can follow to help you pinpoint the funding opportunity:

- **Familiarise yourself with EU funding programmes**: Begin by conducting research on EU funding programmes like Horizon Europe and Erasmus as well as other relevant calls in your field of expertise. Understand their goals, priorities, and target sectors or fields to determine which programmes are most suitable for your project idea. Remember some programmes are not immediately obvious in relation to a research programme, for example Marie Skłodowska-Curie Actions for staff exchanges can provide substantial grants to consortia. Some for us took part in such an exchange (CODEMISUSED) funded at 2 million euros.
- **Evaluate funding calls:** Within each funding programme there may be calls with different themes, priorities, and requirements. Carefully examine the details of each call including eligibility criteria, funding amounts, project duration, and submission deadlines.
- Thoroughly research the level of likely competition within a programme (for example, some programmes in Horizon attract significant numbers of applications compared to others). Such information will give you a clearer idea as to how likely you are to win funding.
- In this context, it is worthwhile seeking a meeting with representatives of the programmes at your national level. They are there to help you and can provide you with such information. Also consult with funding expertise within your organisation (such as research support unit), they often know of programmes that are under-utilised in terms of applications thus increasing your likelihood of winning funding.
- **Thoroughly understand requirements**: Once you have identified a funding opportunity make sure to comprehend the application guidelines set out by the specific funding programme—these can vary considerably, even within broad programmes like Horizon, reflecting the different priorities of a specific Call. These can be very densely written so give yourself time to read through and

comprehend them. This understanding will enable you to tailor your project proposal closely to the guidelines and increase your chances of securing the desired funds.
- **Seek insights from experts**: To enhance your application's appeal consider reaching out to recipients or experts in cognate fields who can provide insights and advice, on how to make an impactful application. If this is your first application, then your national agency/contact point may provide you with funds to hire a professional application writer who can help you write your application. However, if you choose to hire someone like this make sure you have plenty of time in relation to the submission deadline to engage with them. Use of such an expert does not guarantee success, however.
- **Assess the compatibility of your project**: Evaluate how well your project aligns with the objectives and priorities outlined in the funding call. Consider factors such as the goals of your project, its intended audience, expected impact and potential for innovation. Additionally analyse how your project can contribute to cutting-edge solutions as emphasised in the funding call. Assess how sustainable your project's deliverables are beyond its funding. This is now an important area impact in calls, so do not neglect it. The stronger the alignment between your project and the details of the funding call, the greater chances of securing funding.

## 2.4 Initial Activities to Start Formulating the Content of Your Application

Before writing an application there are some key activities you should undertake in terms of formulating its content. These are outlined below:

- **Policy priorities**: To formulate a viable project idea it is crucial to comprehend and align with the policy priorities outlined by each funding programme and specific call. In this regard, remember that the narrative of your project idea must explicitly embrace ALL of the policy priorities outlined in the specific call. We have more to say about this in Sect. 2.3 below.
- **Added value:** Cross reference your project idea with priorities in cognate policy areas—this is important when writing about the **added value** of your project. In the application, you will want to argue that its outcomes extend beyond the specific call to interface with other EU initiatives/policies. Therefore, inform yourself well in advance about these cognate areas
- **Advertise your presence when the call is made**: Research programme guidelines so you are fully informed. Then, participate in call-specific events at which you should ask questions and seek advice from field experts. This will foreground your presence amongst decision makers and stakeholders in the call area at the time (and build relations with them) and help you get a clearer focus on how you need to address the overall goals of the programme within the application.

- **Preliminary depth discussions with your partners**: Before writing an application, you should hold a series of meetings with potential partners to discuss the application. Subjects of discussion should include what the project is about in relation to the Call; negotiating complementary roles, responsibilities, and expectations for each partner in terms of writing the application and project implementation should funding be awarded.
- Discussions should cultivate a shared understanding of the project's aim, objectives, and expectations in relation to the specific call. Through such discussions, you will establish a robust partnership in relation to the specific call but also for future ones.
- **Gathering data about partners**: Once you have identified partners, and they have agreed to join the consortium gather data about them that would be relevant to their participation in the call. This is one of the positive things about EU funding calls. A project track record is not reliant just on the principal lead. Thus, you need to find out from your consortium partners about similar projects with which they and their institutions have been involved or led (if EU funded even better!). You then include these in your narrative of past successes in the call area. In addition, also gather data about your partners' peer-review publications.

As an example, in our funding application for the SSTeMM project (which addressed stress experienced by student nurses when on clinical placement) we gathered data on previous EU-funded projects that members of the consortium had successfully completed in the field of occupational stress (ROSE—Reducing Occupational Stress in Employment); assessing stress and providing education interventions amongst engineers (IMPRESS—Improving management competences on Excellence-based Stress avoidance and working towards Sustainable organisational development in Europe) and providing certified online training in stress management (DELAROSE—Delivering E-Learning Accreditation to Reduce Occupational Stress Employment).

Your consortium's past delivery successes and evidence of same are important to gather for inclusion in your application. Such information will reassure the evaluators that you will not waste money through failure to deliver a commissioned project. However, you need to gather this data well in advance of writing the application for several reasons. The first is that your partners will probably need to contact and get the detail (exact dates, grant code, etc.) of such projects from their respective project offices. This can take time. Second, you need time thoroughly to understand their approach and outcomes to think about how they can enhance your narrative within the application.

### *2.4.1 The Project Card*

Following the above activity, a good way to consolidate and summarise your ideas, align them with a programme call's priorities and objectives, and to communicate what you have learned to your potential consortium partners for their comment is to draw up a Project Card (PC). We have developed the Project Card (PC) format over the last 15 years (we provide the detail of the format in Appendix C) and this can be used as part of the application development process for a wide range of projects.

The idea behind the PC is to summarise and communicate succinctly the initial project idea and structure to all those involved so that they can quickly comprehend the broad detail of such and make suggestions for improvements. The ideal PC offers a short 'bullet point description' of the key elements involved. We recommend the PC should be no more than between 1000 and 1500 words structure under the headings outlined in Appendix C in bullet point format.

Beyond its development advantage, the PC allows all those involved to quickly summarise the project idea, projected involvement of each partner and potential budget to their respective management structures to 'green light' involvement in an application. It also can inform the drawing up mandates/ agreements between partners.

In addition to the structured headings for a PC in Appendix C, you will also find there a link for downloading a PC template.

In the next section we focus in depth on the above as it relates to a specific call process.

## 2.5 Preparing Your Application

Aligning your project with a funding programme's policy priorities and the Call's specific details is very important for securing funding and achieving project success. This section therefore emphasises the significance of demonstrating your understanding of the 'eco-system' of policy priorities contained within a call and establishing a consortium that demonstrates a complementary expertise required to execute your project in relation to such priorities and details.

- **The funding limits:** Usually in an EU programme call the number of projects to be funded in relation to the budget allocation is specifically stated. In relation to funding 'the devil is in the detail', and you can easily misunderstand exactly how the funding mechanism works or what activities it will fund. For example, in a recent call for which we applied—successfully—we misunderstood an important detail in relation to the budget allocation which led us to apply for less funding than we could have been awarded! This misreading of the funding allocation has meant that we have had to undertake some activities at our own cost.
- Sometimes the EU will fund one or two projects beyond this initial announcement (for example, this happened in an emergency HORIZON call during the COVID lockdown in 2020) but it is rare. However, some projects not successful in receiving funding are placed on a reserve list in order of merit should, for some reason, one of the successful project consortia decide not to accept the funding—again this is very rare, but it occasionally happens.

- **Understanding the policy objectives and the detail of the guidelines specific to the Call**: As indicated in Sect. 2.2 EU funding calls are often very densely written, quite long and can seem frustratingly repetitive. This can lead you to miss very important details in relation to a Call. A common mistake when writing an application is not aligning your project narrative with the policy focus of the specific Call because you have missed specific details.
- Therefore, read the Call in which you are interested carefully (and more than once) to gain a comprehensive understanding of the policy objectives specific to the Call. Whilst reading highlight keywords and phrases. These will need to appear within your narrative to demonstrate that you understand the policy objectives.
- Under policy objectives there will often be densely written guidelines. By 'dense', we mean many guidelines. These will state what is expected in your application and what you have to do in the application. There can be a temptation to 'rush' through these because they can feel repetitive and therefore you may feel you know them. Be aware there are in fact subtle differences that you need to be aware of. So again, we recommend that you allow yourself plenty of time to read and comprehend these well in advance of writing the application.
- We also recommend you dedicate sufficient time to review and comprehend the evaluation criteria specific to the Call before starting to write your application. Remember that each funding programme may have its own unique evaluation criteria. Knowing these evaluation criteria will allow you to identify any potential weaknesses in your proposal and address them proactively before submitting your application. Furthermore, knowledge of the evaluation criteria will allow you to tailor your proposal to meet the Call's specific expectations.
- Thus, it is important to visit the official EU websites associated with a specific Call to find accurate and up-to-date evaluation criteria. Also consult with relevant EU institutions or agencies that manage the specific funding opportunities you are interested in.
- One source we highly recommend you is consult the representatives of your local EU national agencies—you will find there are agencies associated with Horizon, Erasmus, and COST to name but a few. They are there to assist you and we have found, for example, the Irish EU national agencies extremely helpful in clarifying elements of a Call and its associated evaluation criteria when we are in the process of writing an application.
- **Gaining an understanding of the Call's policy priorities**: When writing your application, it is essential that you mention explicitly the policy the priorities within the Call. You need to know whether and how they interface with other policy priorities not explicitly mentioned. You also need to know how your project interfaces with all of these. Therefore, take time to review carefully relevant policy documents in cognate policy areas to the Programme and Call.
- Search policy documents from various official sources, for example, the European Commission's Website; European Agency Websites; European Council. Also check national or regional government websites, which may offer access to EU policy documents and guidelines related to project preparation.

- **Tailoring your proposal to priorities**: Once you have a thorough understanding of the policy priorities and specific objectives and requirements of the Call in which you are interested you then need to tailor your project idea to address these specifics.
- As we said earlier, you need to reference explicitly within your application EU policy priorities and documents that the Call cites for its rationale and align your proposal not only with these but with the broader strategic priorities of the European Union. This will demonstrate the contextual relevance of your proposal and ensure that the proposal's goals and expected outcomes align with the funding programme's priorities. Remember, Calls are impact oriented as this relates to policy. Demonstrating both your understanding of policy and your proposal's alignment in progressing policy for impact will make it more compelling to evaluators and increase your chances of securing funding.
- **Establishing a diverse consortium**: Establishing a diverse team with complementary skills and expertise is more likely to address the various complexities inherent within an EU- funded project. Therefore, using your network gather together a consortium of partners with the necessary disciplinary and interdisciplinary knowledge relevant to the Call priorities.
- Do not forget to promote gender balance amongst consortium members. You should aim for a minimum gender balance of 60/40% though of course the best outcome is 50/50%.
- Diversity of geographic/national representation is important within the consortium. The European Union consists of 27 member states and that such diversity of regions and nations should be reflected in the makeup of your consortium. Thus, be mindful that your consortium is not made up of members from one or two nations or regions within the EU. Thus, we aim in our applications to draw consortium members from the western, central, and eastern EU member states.

In addition to the above, the EU also provides free services that you can use to search for partners. Recently, it has established a Funding & Tenders Opportunities Portal that is now the single entry point for finding and managing EU grants. Within this portal, there is a partner search tool that allows you to search for partners who may have expertise that will be useful for your project. You can also use these services to advertise your project idea to attract potential partners to make contact with you.

Depending on the funding programme concerned, national contact points also provide partner search services, offering detailed partner profiles and active partnership requests.

Below is a list, provided by the EU, of information and services for finding partners with expertise in a range of areas:

- Idealist Partner Search—mainly, but not limited to, information and communications technology

- Enterprise Europe Network Cooperation Opportunities database—includes innovation and technology profiles from international companies and research organisations
- Online manual—guidance for finding partners
- Education partners—find partners for EU funding opportunities in education
- European neighbourhood policy—information on funding recipients for neighbourhood policy
- Enterprise Europe Network—helps connect you with international partners

## 2.6 Conclusion

The development of long-term friendly relationships in your field will facilitate you to identify partners who will help you build a solid foundation for your project proposal and, should it get funded, commit to support you in achieving your objectives. Building such relationships over time will maximise your chances of obtaining funding and your project's impact once it has come to an end. To get to such a happy position you need to carry out a thorough evaluation of EU policy in your field of interest. You need to align your project idea with EU policy goals and develop relationships with experts such as your NCP to draw on their expertise as to which are the most aligned calls to apply for in relation to your idea.

**C.-Andreas Dalluege** Founder and Managing Partner of IBK Group; Chairman of the European Business Excellence Network e.V.; National Council Member of the Irish Work Study Institute. Certified Advisor & Trainer of EFQM, Operating Partner and Trainer of Initiative Ludwig-Erhard-Preis (ILEP).

Since 1990 he participated as the senior researcher for his organisation in over 35 EU projects in most programme types offered by the EU and represented his company in all of them at the Management Board level as well as worked as our lead researcher in them.

He serves on the national board of the Irish Work Study Institute (IIESMS) and as President of the European Business Excellence Network (EuroBEN).

As a lecturer at the TH Aschaffenburg, he also gives classes on the design, proposing, and running of EU Research projects since 2019. Contact: cad@ibk.eu

**Dominika Vrbnjak** Associate Professor at the University of Maribor Faculty of Health Sciences is a member of Sigma Theta Tau International, Honour Society of Nursing, the European Academy of Nursing Science, and the International Association of Human Caring. Her research interests include caring and safety and quality in nurse education and practice. She has experience with national and international projects related to pedagogical approaches in nursing and technology in nursing education. Contact: dominika.vrbnjak@um.si

**Majda Pajnkihar** Professor, PhD, RN, FAAN, FEANS, former Dean of the Faculty of Health Sciences, University of Maribor, Head of the Institute of Nursing care, Senior Researcher and Full Professor, who has been involved in numerous national and international projects. Her teaching experience includes work at numerous internationally renowned universities. She is a member of Sigma Theta Tau International, the Honour Society of Nurses and a Fellow of the American

Academy of Nursing and the European Academy of Nursing Sciences. Contact: majda.pajnkihar@um.si

**John Stephen Gary Wells** PhD, FAAN, FNMFRCSI (Ad Eundem) is Dean of the School of Health Sciences at the South East Technological University. John graduated from the University of Manchester with a degree in history. Following graduation, he trained and practised as a mental health nurse in London, eventually managing one of the busiest acute psychiatric admission units in the capital. John then transitioned from a clinical practice role to an academic one in 1993, moving to Ireland in 1998 to take up an academic position there.

John is an active and experienced researcher. As either Principal Investigator or co-investigator he has won funding from national and EU-funded research programmes to the value of 12 million Euros. He is a member of the National Research Ethics Committee for Clinical Trials in Ireland and holds visiting professorships at UCD, Ireland, King's College London, UK, and Maribor University, Slovenia. John has published 115 peer-reviewed papers, 7 technical reports (commissioned by regional, national, and EU agencies), 9 book chapters, and 1 book.

At the time of publication he is principal investigator for an EU4Health-funded project on enhancing the digital skills of the pan-European health care workforce. He is also chairperson of a COST Action on expanding the access of people with intellectual disabilities to cancer services. Contact: john.wells@setu.ie

# Chapter 3
# Writing Your Application and Navigating the EU Submission Process

**C.-Andreas Dalluege, Florian Scheibein, Gregor Štiglic, and John Stephen Gary Wells**

Writing your application and navigating the EU submission process can be challenging for applicants, particularly those who are new to the process or have limited experience with grant applications. This chapter provides guidance on some of the key aspects of writing an application in response to an EU programme Call that provides evaluators with a clear and compelling narrative for funding. It also provides guidance on portal management and how to deal with some of the challenges that can arise in the online submission process.

Some of the key challenges you need to think about in writing your application include:

- **Writing a compelling proposal**: As we outlined in Chap. 2, writing a proposal that clearly demonstrates your project's value and impact that aligns with the funding programme's priorities is a challenging task. It requires strong writing skills, a deep understanding of your project's objectives and benefits as these relate to all the priorities laid out in the programme Call, and the ability to communicate these effectively to evaluators.
- **Managing complex application requirements:** EU-funded projects often have complex application requirements, including detailed project descriptions of budgets, work plans, and provision of supporting documentation. Navigating

C.-A. Dalluege
IBK, Wiesbaden, Germany
e-mail: cad@ibk.eu

F. Scheibein · J. S. G. Wells (✉)
South East Technological University, Waterford, Ireland
e-mail: Florian.Scheibein@setu.ie; john.wells@setu.ie

G. Štiglic
University Maribor, Maribor, Slovenia
e-mail: gregor.stiglic@um.si



C.-A. Dalluege, J. S. G. Wells (eds.), *Navigating an EU Research Project*, Management for Professionals, https://doi.org/10.1007/978-3-031-70928-9_3

these requirements and ensuring that your proposal meets these requirements can be a daunting and personally as well as institutionally resource-intensive process.
- **Navigating the EU submission portal:** The EU submission portal can be complicated to navigate, particularly for first-time users. The portal tends not to be intuitive and have complexities that are not immediately obvious when you engage with it. Exploring and understanding the portal platform's functionality and requirements before you fill in the required application fields therefore is crucial to ensure a smooth submission process and avoid/manage technical issues that could jeopardise your application.
- **Meeting strict deadlines:** The EU submission process often involves tight deadlines for submitting proposals and required documentation. Ensuring that all necessary materials are prepared and submitted on time (preferably well in advance of the submission deadline) can be a challenging and time-consuming task, especially when coordinating with multiple partners within your consortium. You need therefore to factor this into your plan for submission—it is not advisable to leave submission to the last day of the deadline. Factor in a day or two prior to the deadline date to deal with unforeseen problems that can arise when you submit.

Below we discuss the above points in more detail.

## 3.1 EU Proposal Evaluators and Addressing What They Look for

Specialist evaluator panels assess and score applications for EU calls. EU evaluator panels typically consist of experts drawn from across member states. The pan-European nature of an evaluation panel means that English, the "second" language most widely spoken across the EU (and one of the official languages of the EU) is the language used by the EU for the purposes of an application. We advise, therefore, that you include a "native" speaker of English as part of the writing team for the application.

The United Kingdom, post Brexit, is eligible to take part in the Horizon programme as a third country (that is, they can participate but cannot be the lead country in an application). However, the UK has opted not to participate in other EU programmes, such as Erasmus. Therefore, if you have a UK partner in a Horizon programme we suggest you include them as a member of the application writing team. Countries within the EU who can take part in all programmes, as lead or as a partner, and one may say, are native speakers of English, post Brexit, include Ireland, Malta, and Cyprus.

It is important to remember that English for most evaluators will be their second language. Therefore, you need to bear this in mind when writing your proposal. Use clear unambiguous words, avoid complex sentences, and minimise technical jargon (use technical jargon only when there is no plain English alternative). We recommend you use the Flesch Reading Ease Scale—an online tool to check your English narrative clarity. This web address—https://plainenglish.ie/readability-test/—provides further information.

In addition to using online scales to check your written English clarity, if you are based in a country where English is not its first language, we recommend that you identify a native speaker employed by your institution to read your application. Most academic institutions within the EU employ native speakers of English in some capacity—academic or administrative. We suggest you identify and contact these individuals.

### *3.1.1 What EU Proposal Evaluators Look for in an Application*

EU proposal evaluators determine which projects should receive funding by scoring them against a set of criteria. These criteria can vary from programme call to programme call. There are, nevertheless, general areas that evaluators look for in assessing proposals that do not vary. It is therefore important to understand what evaluators prioritise generally as it can enhance your chances of success.

- **Alignment with programme objectives and priorities:** Evaluators look for projects that directly align with the stated objectives and priorities outlined in the funding call. It is essential to demonstrate how your project meets these criteria and emphasise its contribution towards achieving programme goals. One of the ways to do this is to use (reflect) the words in the funding call within your application to demonstrate alignment.
- **Quality of the consortium and its management:** When considering the quality of a consortium and its project management, evaluators take into account the qualifications, experience, and expertise of the project partners. Before we look at these, however, we need to remind you of two consortium elements, which we indicated earlier in Chap. 2 to which you need to pay close attention when building your consortium. The first is gender balance—you need to aim for a gender balance amongst all individuals that make up your consortium a minimum of 40/60% between the sexes though obviously the ideal would be a 50%/50% division. Second, try and build a consortium that includes partners from the west, east, north, and south of the EU.
- It's essential to demonstrate the track record of your consortium and explain how each partners' skills will contribute to the project's overall success. We address how you should write about this in the application form in more detail in Sect. 3.2.2 below.
- **Excellence and innovation:** Evaluators highly value projects that showcase approaches, test ground-breaking ideas, or develop and test cutting-edge interventions or technologies. Highlight these aspects of your project and explain how they advance practices or address existing knowledge gaps referenced to the

call. It would be beneficial to include real-life examples that demonstrate how your project will tackle these. Such highlighting will make your application stand out compared to others.

- **Impact and sustainability:** Evaluators assess not only the impact of your project deliverables on a target audience, sector, or region but also its long-term sustainability. Clearly outlining the expected outcomes and benefits of your project for the target sector while emphasising how it will create lasting change beyond the funded implementation period is crucial. Over the last few years, the weighting of this in the scoring of an application has steadily increased within the assessment criteria used by evaluators. It is perhaps the most challenging part of an application and argued closely, with supporting evidence, particularly calling upon your consortium's past successes. We provide more detail about this in Chap. 8, Sect. 8.2 below.
- **Risk mitigation:** Evaluators appreciate projects that acknowledge risks and challenges while proposing strategies to address them. It is important to be transparent, about any obstacles you anticipate and explain how you plan to overcome them for project execution. We describe the general principles and some detail when developing your risk mitigation in Chap. 5, Sect. 5.6 below.
- **Methodology and work plan:** Evaluators look for structured, logical, and feasible work plans that include tasks, milestones, and deliverables. Evaluators will assess whether your work plan is practical and attainable, taking into account the scale of the project and available resources against the proposed timelines. Therefore, it is very important that you are not tempted to over promise on processes and delivery in relation to the resources you are requesting, or the resource limits imposed by the Call. Evaluators will in general mark your proposal as unrealistic in relation to the work plan and available timelines and resources if you "over" promise. We discuss the matching of resources to your work plan in more detail in Sect. 3.4.1 below.
- **Budget:** Evaluators closely analyse budget allocation to ensure that funds are used effectively. As we have indicated in the preceding sections, it is important that you provide a clear budget that justifies all costs in relation to project activities and objectives. We address budgeting in more detail in Sect. 3.2.4 below.
- **Communication and dissemination:** Evaluators will assess how you plan to communicate/ disseminate your project's results to your proposed target audience/ sector and the wider audience of stakeholders implied within a Call. Remember your communication/dissemination plan and its implementation is not discreet within itself, but a significant aspect of project impact. You need to emphasise, therefore, its relationship to your impact strategy.
- Within your application, therefore, you need to explain clearly how you will do this to ensure your results effectively reach your proposed audience and what impact you expect your communication/ dissemination strategy to have both during the funded project and post funding. You need to provide minimum metrics against which to measure the success of your strategy. We recommend that when writing about post-funded project impact, you include open access/open science principles and how your project will promote these.

- **Promoting cooperation across the EU and beyond**: Evaluators also assess how your project adds value to pan-European integration and cooperation within your field of interest. In your narrative emphasise collaboration across borders. Describe the representativeness and collaboration between your partners in your consortium and, in turn, their network reach.
- Next, describe how your project promotes knowledge exchange and cooperation among researchers, experts, and professionals across Europe. Describe how it will facilitate the sharing of best practices and innovative solutions that provide benefits beyond the funded lifetime of the project. Also, show how the project will integrate results with previous or concurrent projects within cognate fields.
- **Aligning with and being sensitive to broader EU policies:** When evaluating your project, the evaluator will consider EU policy aspects such as data protection (GDPR) and environmental impact (the European Green Deal). It is crucial to ensure that your project adheres to such policies, particularly, as in the case of GDPR. Also, don't forget to address issues of intellectual property rights should these be a feature of your project and how they interface with data protection and principles of open access.
- Where there is policy, but little in the way of legislative requirements (such as the European Green Deal), it is still important to demonstrate sensitivity to aligning your application to the spirit of such policy. For example, when justifying face-to-face consortium meetings (we are great supporters of holding some meetings face-to-face for relationship building and strategic planning purposes) justify their importance and describe how consortium partners will travel to and from these in a manner, where possible, that will reduce the consortium's carbon footprint.

In summary when evaluating EU proposals evaluators will look for alignment with the call objectives and demonstration of innovative impacts interfacing with post project sustainability, underpinned by a realistic methodology, a credible consortium to deliver on what you promise and a clear, realistic, and justified budget allocation. Clarity of narrative is key to making a convincing case that your project is worth funding.

## 3.2 Writing Your Application

As we indicated in Chap. 2, EU application forms have character (not word) limits that you cannot exceed. These are set as defaults within the online application form. Nothing else you write on the form beyond the set limit will appear on the application form. Therefore, we have found that the use of graphics rather than narrative can communicate material that, if included in the narrative, would "crowd out" other narrative you need to include because of the character limits.

For example, we have extensive networks that we cite as part of our dissemination and impact narrative. For us to list these narratively would probably take up the entire application form's character limits. However, as you see from the graphical representation below (Fig. 3.1), we articulate our networks and show their relationships with one another in relation to our dissemination and impact strategy in picture format. This example is from our recent successful application in response to a Call issued by the EU for Health initiative. This project, DDS-MAP, started in Spring, 2023.

### 3.2.1 *Writing About the Alignment of Your Project Objectives with Call Priorities, Impact, and Sustainability*

When outlining your desired objectives and the timeline, for achieving them it is important to be specific both internally, in relation to your project's overall aim, and externally, with the Call priorities. It is surprising how many times we have seen applications in which there are very specific and well-written objectives that are misaligned with the overall stated goal of a project and when tested against a Call's overall strategic priorities are difficult to trace a relationship.

We suggest you integrate the precise words used in the Call within your overall project aim and in your project's specific objectives. This will act to foreground the

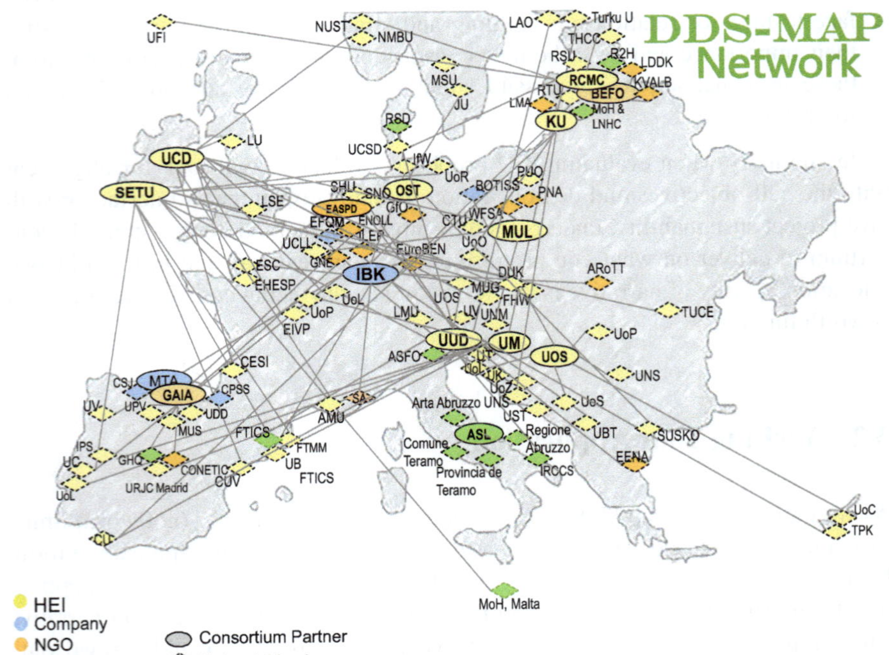


**Fig. 3.1** Example of Consortium Network Illustrating potential dissemination and impact cooperation partners beyond the immediate consortium members

Call priorities in your planning and in your application narrative; thereby ensuring there is no misalignment.

While articulating your project objectives in the application it is essential to anticipate, and state, challenges or obstacles that may arise during implementation and say describe your plans to address them. You should discuss these with your partners in a planning meeting prior to writing your application, as there may be issues that you are not aware of that they have seen.

It is very important that you state these issues honestly within your application; and how you plan to mitigate them. Remember, when a funded project comes to an end the EU evaluators will assess and score its success against what you said you would do in your original application. If your project is marked as below what you stated you would do in your application, the EU is entitled to ask for its money back!

It is also beneficial to consider and discuss with your partners the expected impact of the project. As we stated earlier impact, both short-term (i.e. impact during a project's lifetime) and long-term (i.e. impact beyond the project's lifetime) is now a significant consideration for evaluators. To maximise the long-term impact of your project it is important to plan for your project's continuity beyond the funding period. It is surprising how often this aspect is neglected or left to the last minute in relation to an application. It should be at the forefront of your thinking, particularly as it can be challenging to think about how you will demonstrate measurement of sustainable impacts POST the funded element of your project.

We suggest that you collectively identify with your partners measurable indicators that accurately reflect your consortium's real-world capabilities in relation to impact—both short- and long-term. Some impact aspects that you should consider with your partners include:

- Do you have sufficient representation within your consortium, such as sector associations, relevant trade unions, or key market partners in relation to the impacts the Programme Call states it wants funded projects to achieve?
- Are your target numbers ambitious enough to leverage opportunities and achieve the impacts you say you want to achieve?
- Have you developed a plan to manage risks and ensure that you achieve stated outcomes? (we go further into detail about this in Chap. 5, Sect. 5.6 below)?
- What opportunities to develop strategic products or processes could arise from your deliverables?
- Could there be further development or expansion of the deliverable once it is implemented?
- What opportunities are there for strategic development of international contacts and sustainable networks once the project is completed?
- Are there forums available through which you can co-operate based on your project experiences that will facilitate your consortium to share deliverables with other projects, sectors, and wider society?
- Can establish and expand commercial distribution channels (where appropriate)?

Your sustainability approach in relation to impacts may involve securing further funding and devising a plan for scaling up the project deliverables. Alternatively, it might involve ensuring that the project's outcomes are sustained and integrated into established systems or practices. For example, in one of our projects—DELAROSE—we emphasised its long-term impact and sustainability by stating that one of our deliverables would be to produce a certificated programme that would be delivered by the participating educational partners within our consortium. This was done (the programme is now 10 years old, has been further developed, and is still being delivered). Data relating to the professionals who have undertaken the programme and from which sectors of health, social care, and other industries they come is available.

### 3.2.2 *Writing About the Quality of Your Consortium:*

As we indicate above representing your consortium in terms of their connectivity to other networks is a powerful way to illustrate their quality. There are other key elements to write about to emphasise your consortium's expertise and quality in relation to the Call:

- **Demonstrate Consortium expertise**—Demonstrating your consortia's expertise is a critical factor for the success of your application. The stated expertise and experience of your consortia directly demonstrates credibility, trust, and sustainability in terms of how you will carry out your project, its likelihood of success, and the delivery of impacts beyond its funded lifetime. You need to be explicit and provide examples, in relation to all these elements.
- As we indicated in Sect. 3.1, EU project evaluation criteria often include an assessment of the project team's qualifications, record, and relevant experience. Capacity and the role of individuals and institutions within your consortium and the extent to which the consortium brings together the necessary expertise to achieve your stated deliverables are evaluated. So, make sure you emphasise your consortium members' individual and complementary skills, experience, and qualifications to prove that you have the capacity to successfully implement the proposed project and achieve meaningful results.
- Carefully highlight their experience or achievements to demonstrate their competence in the subject matter. It is also important to emphasise how complementary expertise within the consortium aligns with the specific requirements of the Call. The following are what you should provide in your application as examples of the quality of the institutional and individual partner's record of success and credibility.
- **Outline a track record of related project successes—**As we said in Sect. 2.4, a track record of previously completed projects in cognate areas, particularly ones that were funded by the EU, goes a long way to demonstrate your consortium's competence and expertise for the specific Call and the delivery of outcomes. A track record serves to give comfort to the funders, such as the EU, that they are not risking their money when awarding it to your consortium.

- Therefore, it is important to outline your team's experience with previous projects as they relate to your current proposal's topic and goals, emphasising the outcomes and achievements of each project. Include information about the project's scope, objectives, methods, and results and explain how this experience is applied to your current proposed project.
- When citing your previous EU-funded projects always provide the award reference code, don't just give the title of the project. If there is an active website associated with the project (which is one way to demonstrate its impact beyond its funded lifetime), then provide the web address.
- In the case of the SSTeMM project proposal for example, as previously mentioned in Sect. 2.3 we cited three previously EU-funded projects in cognate areas in which members of the consortium had either led or participated in (ROSE, DELAROSE, and IMPRESS). We explained the impacts of each project and how their achieved outcomes would inform are progression of SSTeMM should it be funded. We also pointed to the fact that IMPRESS had an active website and set of stress assessment tools that we could employ and build upon in SSTeMM. In relation to DELAROSE we cited a set of certified programmes on stress management that had been established as a result of that project. We stated that we could adapt and further develop these programmes within the SSTeMM project.
- Discussing trans-sectoral expertise within the consortium, based on your consortium's previous projects, demonstrates the "added value" of your current proposal; that is, you make explicit that whilst your project focuses on a specific sector, what you deliver may have value for other sectors as demonstrated by previous projects.
- For example, within the SSTeMM project whilst we developed tools for individual stress management of student nurses, our survey assessment approach could also be applied to conduct an anonymous aggregated assessment in many sectors to inform an organisation about the existing or upcoming common areas of stress within their workforce so they can address these before they become a problem.
- **Showcase publications and research:** Several team members will have already published research or articles related to the subject of your application. Be sure to mention these in your application. However, be strategic in relation to the publication record you cite—long citations can quickly eat into the application form's character limits.
- Citing articles published by members of the consortium demonstrates your consortium's commitment to the field and provides evidence of their expertise. When listing these references, they can include titles that have only a tangential relationship to your proposal's core topic as such references also show your overall research competence and potential for extending results to cognate sectors.
- **Awards and recognitions:** If members of the consortium or their institutions have received awards, grants, or other recognition for their work related to your application, include this information. This can help to establish your consortium's credibility and reinforce its expertise in the field.

- For example, in the case of our SSTeMM project these not only touched stress management topics but included international recognised competence of one partner on the topic of Business Excellence and what businesses needed for assessing potential stress factors and resources.
- **Emphasise relevant qualifications:** Highlight relevant qualifications and certifications of your consortium members, such as degrees, professional certifications, or specialised training in relation to the programme Call and your application. This will help to demonstrate individual competence and ability to contribute to the proposed project.
- **Include testimonials and references:** If possible, include testimonials or references from collaborators or beneficiaries of your past projects. These endorsements can provide further evidence of your consortium's expertise and the impact of their work in the field of interest.

By showcasing your consortium's track record, in our example in stress management projects, you establish your credibility and expertise in the field. Evaluators will be more confident in your ability to successfully implement and manage your project. Your team's demonstrated experience with publications and networking will also further enhance your credibility in terms of sustainable impact of the project results in their post—funding project use—an issue that has become of more importance over the recent Call cycles.

### *3.2.3 Writing About Governance, Risk Management, and Risk Mitigation Within Your Application*

Your application needs to outline confidently a strong governance structure that describes decision-making processes, communication channels, and conflict resolution mechanisms (we deal with this in more detail in Chap. 5). You should explain how your governance structures will ensure that the consortium functions effectively and can adapt to any challenges or changes that may arise during the project's trajectory. Having a convincing but not over-bureaucratic project-management structure is an evaluation criterion for all projects, so check with other successful projects what was considered as state-of-the-art governance structures and adapt these to your current proposal.

Also describe how you will formalise your partnership by developing a written agreement that outlines the terms of collaboration, roles and responsibilities, financial arrangements, and any other relevant details. Many EU programmes request that applicants have such a consortium agreement in place in addition to the formal contract with the relevant EU Project Office if your project should get funding. We provide more detail on contracts in Chap. 4.

A significant element within a project governance structure is communication channels between partners within the consortium. You should describe how you will encourage regular communication between partners in relation to updates on your project's progress and which partners have a specific role in the project in relation to communicating with others in the consortium on specific aspects for which they are responsible. For the purposes of writing your application, use graphical representations of communication strategy with a short narrative explanation. It is an area that lends itself well to a graphic and thereby saves you breaching character limits. (See Chap. 5, where we describe in detail communication structures and approaches in more detail).

Recognise within the narrative of your application that partnerships may evolve over time. Describe how you plan to accommodate potential changes or contingencies. This might include adding project advisors, adjusting roles and responsibilities, or addressing conflicts that arise during the project's implementation.

This leads us into writing about your risk management plan. Most funding programmes ask you to consider risk potentials and state how you will deal with them if they appear. As part of your application narrative, it is important to define what constitutes a risk. For example, we define "Risk" as an uncertainty that if it materialises could affect costs, timelines, and deliverables of your project.

Some examples of risks include the potential for delays between an award of a grant and the ability to start a project. Increased administrative and coordination efforts to meet EU reporting requirements or delayed cash flow for expenses spent against funds received.

This concept of uncertainty can influence relationships within a consortium and prove to act as tension points between people that may also need to be managed. However, whilst "risk" can pose a threat to a project, it can also facilitate opportunities (see Fig. 3.2) that prompt you to do things differently.

As part of your narrative, it is important to explain your risk management strategy as both a mitigation approach and as a platform to facilitate adaptive change as your project proceeds. In this narrative you need to identify risks. Explain how this strategy will enable your consortium to handle any foreseen challenges and minimise their impact, on the success of the project. Acknowledge that you cannot be expected to cover all challenges when outlining risks and mitigations, but state that you have identified the likely ones to arise and have a sufficiently flexible risk management approach to deal with unforeseen challenges.

It is worth articulating in the risk management section of your application how you or one of your consortium partners have gained insights from completed projects in relation to managing risks. For example, in future applications we will reference our expansion of risk management experience based on mitigating impacts on the SSTeMM project during the "Covid lockdown".

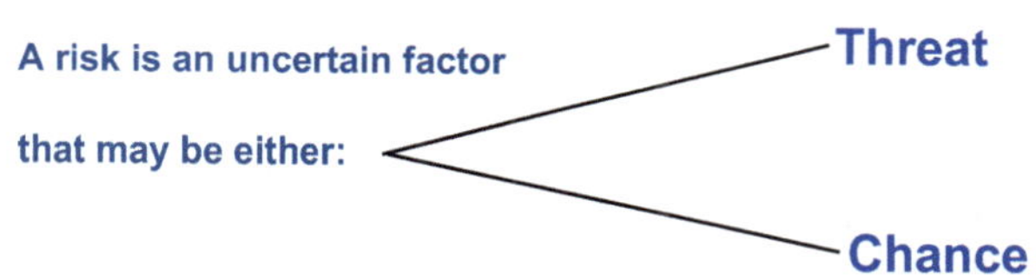


Fig. 3.2 Risk types

So, within your application, you should write a narrative that covers at a minimum the following items:

- Anticipated risks
- Assessing their impacts
- Defining appropriate responses to address these issues.

Some funding Calls require that you list risks within a table format. Table 3.1 below is an example of such a tabular list of risks.

In relation to the management of risk more broadly it is important to articulate how you intend to consistently monitor the progress of your project, in relation to its goals and how you will go about making adjustments to achieve goals should this prove necessary. This reassures the EU evaluator that your project will stay on course and will adapt effectively to any changes or challenges that may arise during its implementation.

**Table 3.1** Potential risk able from an ERASMUS+ proposal

| Risk No | Description | WP No | Proposed risk-mitigation measures |
|---|---|---|---|
| 1 | Difficulties to settle problems via online communication<br>Risk: low | All | Planning of face-to- face meetings |
| 2 | Non-performer among partners<br>Risk: low | All | Risk Management measures according to Project Manual |
| 3 | Pandemic risk of new travel bans<br>Risk: low | All | In case a new virus variant will cause a revival of reduced personal contacts and a new restriction of travel we will increase the number of virtual meetings to balance this. |
| 4 | Partner not delivering timesheets and progress summaries on time<br>Risk: low | WP1 | Fixed time lines to ensure delivery is continually monitored; followed up by coordinating partner |
| 5 | Underlying Excellence Model not adapted correctly due to missing in-depth knowledge<br>Risk: medium | WP2 | Process will be coordinated by the partner who is both a certified Advisor and Trainer for EFQM and who could run an EFQM Training for all if so needed |
| 6 | Training materials "too shallow" or "too academic" to catch the interest of people<br>Risk: low | WP3 | Having both HEI and VET experts in the consortium who are experts in developing fitting training modules |
| 7 | Companies/organisations cannot carry out pilot projects in the planned time<br>Risk: low | WP4 | To attract more companies for the piloting process to be utmost flexible |
| 8 | Delays in linking up the project relevant platforms of the national, European, and international network<br>Risk: medium | WP5 | Definition of common approach right from project start. Ensure the correct dissemination and exploitation of the project results. |

### 3.2.4 Writing Your Work Plan and Balancing Resource Allocation with Partner Task Allocation

To enhance the credibility of your application it is important to develop a work plan that outlines a sequence of tasks, milestones, and deliverables. Make sure your plan is realistic and feasible within the scope of the Call versus the resources you request and the timeline for the project. Do not over promise what you will do—remember the EU will hold you to that promise in terms of the work schedule and the deliverables.

In developing your work plan, as the project coordinator (this is the common term used for the lead partner in an EU-funded project), it is important that you clearly define the respective roles and responsibilities of each of your partners within the application form as this relates to task input. Outline your partners' specific tasks and contributions to the project. These should reflect their specific skill sets and be demonstrated in the work allocation format within your application (for example, time and funding allocated to each partner for specific roles and tasks). Describe the complementarities of partners' skill sets and expertise for the achievement of specific outcomes.

As we stated when we discussed the establishment of diversity and balance within your consortium, you need to be mindful that your work and funding allocation does not overly favour one or two partners over others in the consortium. For example, in Fig. 3.3 below we provide a real example of a partner's work to funding calculation, taken from a real proposal to demonstrate what we mean.

You can see that the German partner within this consortium had a total of under 30% of labour, but due to given labour rates they received 43% of the funding—this was seen by the EU evaluators as unbalanced and was a main reason why the project scored technically good, but was not funded.

When presenting your work plan you need to demonstrate a careful consideration of practical implementation aspects. For reference purposes you can include aids such as GANTT charts or PERT charts (Figs. 3.4 and 3.5). These are commonly

| | | | RLS | UoS | SCIPA | IBK | BEFO | WCC | AHRL | RDAO | |
|---|---|---|---|---|---|---|---|---|---|---|---|
| | | Partners | RLS | UoS | SCIPA | IBK | BEFO | WCC | AHRL | RDAO | |
| | | Member state | DE | HR | RO | DE | LV | IE | LV | RO | |
| | | Average Person Day costs | 195,05 | 66,25 | 66,25 | 195,1 | 66,25 | 218 | 66,25 | 66,25 | sums |
| PM | Project & Quality Management | PersDays | fixed | fixed | fixed | fixed | fixed | fixed | fixed | fixed | 0 |
| | | Total Cost for WP | 28.750 | 13.025 | 13.025 | 13.025 | 13.025 | 13.025 | 13.025 | 13.025 | 119.925 |
| IO1 | Underlying methodology ... | 4 | 83 | 88 | 53 | 124 | 69 | 39 | 39 | 39 | 534 |
| | | Total Cost for WP | 17.398 | 6.360 | 3.846 | 26.068 | 5.011 | 9.195 | 2.810 | 2.810 | 73.498 |
| IO2 | Ttraining material ... | 2 | 105 | 197 | 93 | 28 | 181 | 58 | 46 | 65 | 773 |
| | | Total Cost for WP | 22.002 | 14.255 | 6.730 | 5.888 | 13.090 | 13.723 | 3.309 | 4.696 | 83.693 |
| IO3 | Validated solution platform | 1 | 201 | 111 | 70 | 58 | 43 | 90 | 90 | 90 | 753 |
| | | Total Cost for WP | 48.826 | 8.424 | 5.466 | 12.152 | 3.125 | 22.031 | 7.289 | 7.289 | 114.602 |
| | | Total Person/Days | 389 | 396 | 216 | 210 | 293 | 187 | 175 | 194 | 2.060 |
| | | Labour costs | 81.426 | 28.639 | 15.642 | 44.108 | 21.226 | 44.149 | 12.608 | 13.995 | 261.793 |
| | | Total Budget | 124.391 | 45.144 | 32.147 | 60.213 | 46.685 | 61.054 | 29.513 | 30.900 | 430.047 |
| | | Labour Distribution in % | 18,9% | 19,2% | 10,5% | 10,2% | 14,2% | 9,1% | 8,5% | 9,4% | 100,0% |
| | | Funding Distribution in % | 28,9% | 10,5% | 7,5% | 14,0% | 10,9% | 14,2% | 6,9% | 7,2% | 100,0% |

**Fig. 3.3** Labour Calculation Overview

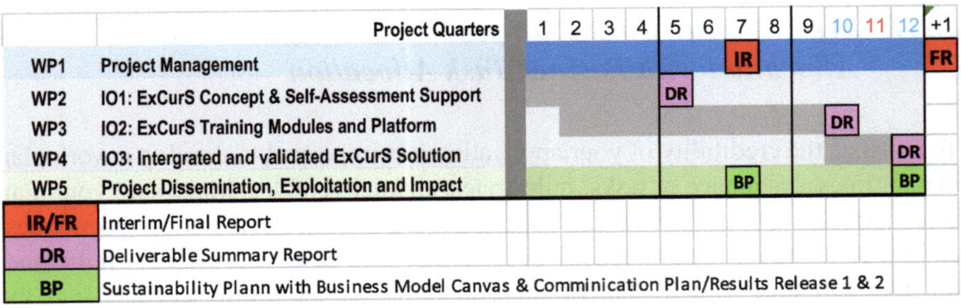


**Fig. 3.4** Project condensed GANTT

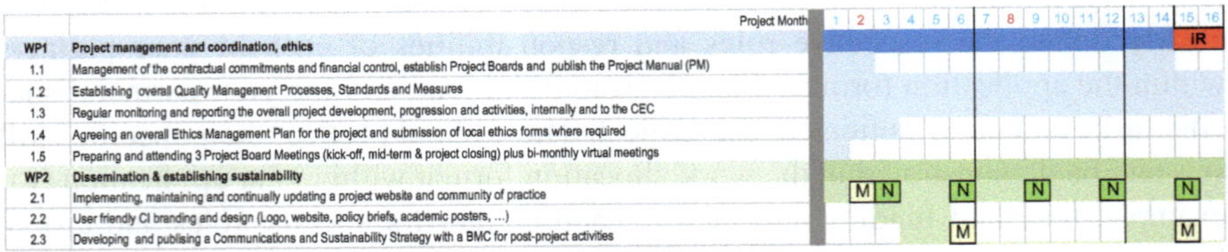

**Fig. 3.5** Project PERT (Programme Evaluation & Review Technique)

used in project proposals to illustrate the schedule and dependencies of the projects. In fact some Calls even request the submission of a detailed GANTT (Fig. 3.6).

You should incorporate milestone progress indicators across the trajectory of your project within your work plan and application narrative. This will indicate to the evaluator how you intend to monitor project progress in relation to delivery of the promised outcomes. Providing progress milestones will provide you with a narrative framework, should your project be funded, for your interim and final progress reports to the EU funding agency.

## 3.3 Articulating Any Intellectual Property Rights Within Your Application

If your proposal involves a product or outcome that involves intellectual property rights (IPR), it is important to highlight this and how it will be managed in your application form. Remember, the general default position of the EU is that if a project receives EU funding then its "products" must be freely available. In these circumstances, therefore, it is important to consult with your NCP for a particular Call as to what is allowed in relation to IPR.

If IPR is allowable within a Call, then outlining its management in your application is important. IPR may arise from individual contributions by partners or from their collaborative efforts. Therefore, it is crucial to define which aspects of a deliverable/deliverables each partner contributes and how these components can be used individually and collectively in relation to IPR.

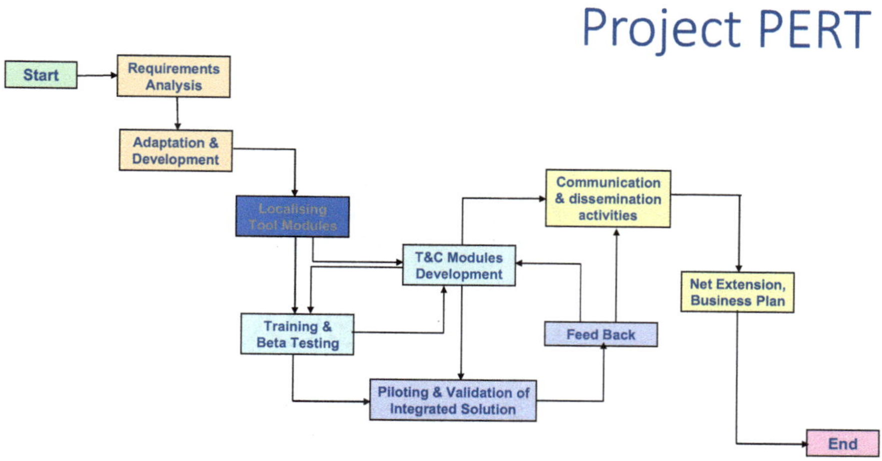


**Fig. 3.6** Detailed GANTT (Excerpt)

The maxim of "as open as possible, as closed as necessary" should guide decisions about IPR and making project outputs available. In this regard, the Creative Commons Licence system is free and relatively easy to understand. Platforms such as Open Science Framework and Zenodo can be used to publish project outputs using this framework. Creative Commons Licences can also be communicated by text (for example, "This work is licensed under CC BY 4.0") and the use of logos (see Fig. 3.7). A "CC0" licence is a licence that enables anyone to use the project output in whatever way they want without crediting the original producer. When "BY" is added to a licence, this means that the output must always be credited to the original producer. "SA" means that any adaptations of the output must be shared under the same licensing terms. "NC" means that the output can only be used for non-commercial purposes. "ND" means non-derivative meaning that no derivatives can be made of the output.

Figure 3.8 illustrates how both existing (GOA = Group Opinion Analyser) and new content within a project we were involved with—the Work Life Flow (WLF) project—synergistically worked together to achieve desired outcomes within timeframes and available resources. This aspect holds significance in programmes where there is an expectation that funded results are accessible at no cost. Failure to define this in advance during proposal development or include it as part of the project contract could result in having to give away materials that required time and resources outside of the project itself.

Figure 3.9 demonstrates how a cascade of Intellectual Property Rights (IPRs) would arise for a product, like GOA-based Stress Assessment tool derived from the SSTeMM Project

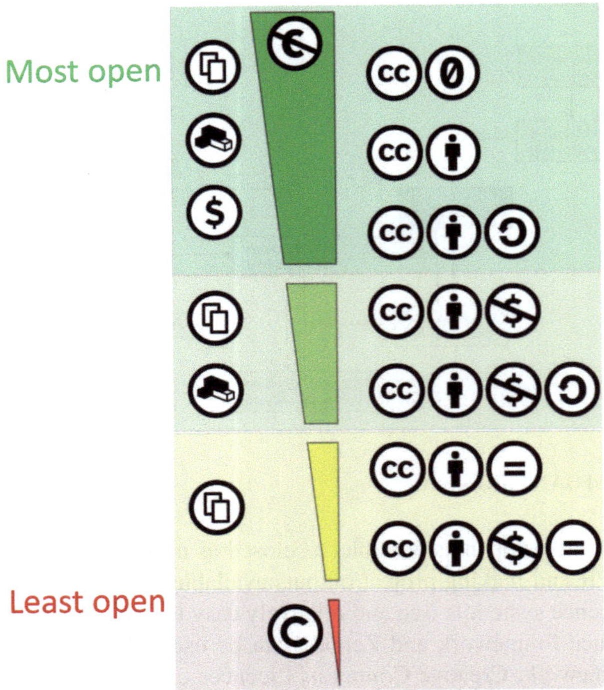


**Fig. 3.7** The trajectory from open to closed IPR (Source: Creative Commons)

## 3.4 Calculating Budgets, Work Packages, and Obtaining Mandates

As we indicated a balanced budget distribution across your consortium is important. A well-structured budget illustrates the financial feasibility and efficient allocation of resources. You need to present a budget that clearly justifies how resources and funding are allocated between partners; this is especially important since the budget and its distribution between partners and specific project outputs as described in the application will become a fixed issue for the running of your project should it be funded. Any substantive errors in the budget outlined in your application, once the project is funded, are generally not allowed to be readjusted as we found in relation to our DDS-MAP project.

Your budget should outline estimated expenses, for personnel, materials, equipment, and subsistence for any face-to-face meetings or attendance of projected conferences, etc. Within your budget narrative, you should outline how you intend to monitor and possibly adjust budget allocations to accommodate any small changes that may arise across the timeline of your project.

Should you be awarded funding, it is not unusual to make small changes to a budget allocation between partners in relation to challenges or changes of task

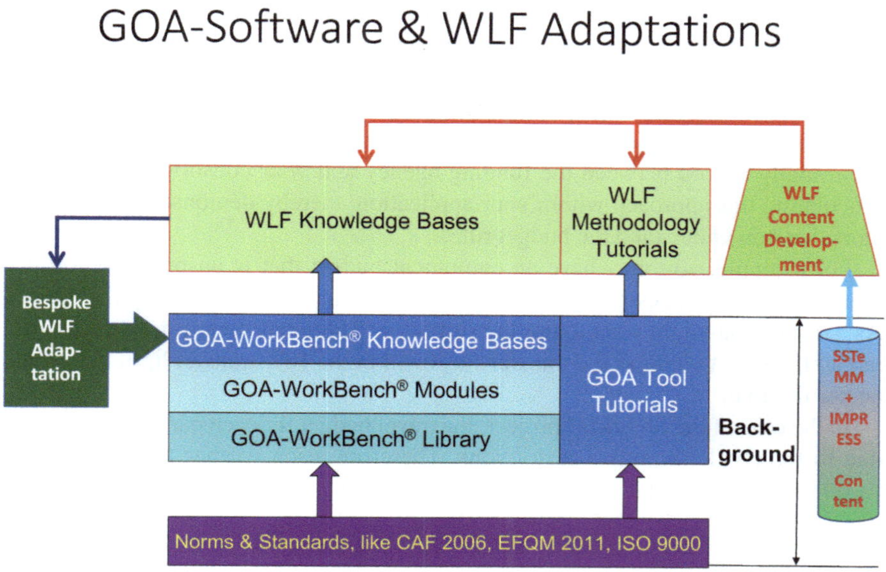


**Fig. 3.8** Inter-linkage project development materials in the context of the Work-Live-Flow project

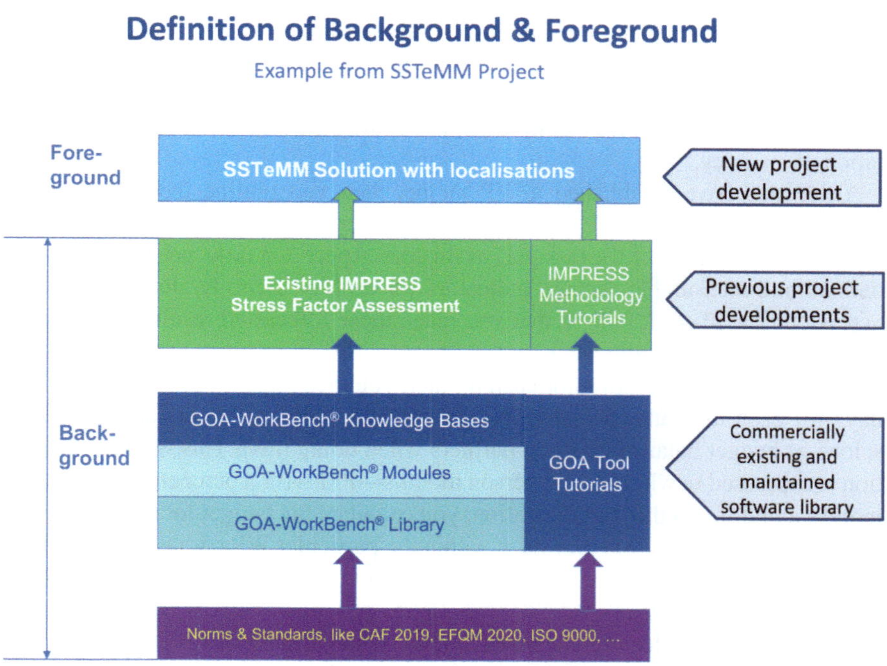


**Fig. 3.9** Example of background and foreground materials within the SSteMM Project

allocation that arise as a project is implemented. However, EU programmes will place limits on how much you can reallocate and generally require that you seek permission from the funding agency beforehand. Most funding programmes have a "10% rule" that allows each partner to reallocate up to 10% of their individual budget at their own discretion to another activity. Any budget transfer above this must be formally agreed between the funding agency and your consortium. It is worth articulating this approach within your application, thereby demonstrating to evaluators that you understand the budget rules.

For example, you may have an equipment budget that is unspent due to price reductions between designing the budget and the actual purchase during the project. As a result, you might want to use the surplus as additional support for your project labour budget. As long as the transfer stays within the 10% transfer limit this would be permissible.

In the case of the SSTeMM project, the travel budget for each partner was unused due to the pandemic travel restrictions. Therefore, each partner transferred their travel budget to their labour cost to address pandemic delays.

### *3.4.1 Work Packages*

In relation to budget planning and allocation, one usually divides one's project into work packages (WP). Work packages are themed around core elements of your project—for example, a governance WP is standard followed by particular WPs for delivery of an outcome, for example a WP may be the development and implementation of a survey.

Once you have established a WP theme, then you outline the specific tasks involved to achieve the WP deliverable. The main cost item in this context is the labour effort for each of the task. EU evaluators expect 3–5 tasks per WP with well-defined and measurable success indicators for each of them. Evaluators will then assess on how likely it will be that you reach these forecasted results based on the labour costs you have allocated.

Following task allocation for each partner, you then allocate how many working days for each task and their distribution between partners (remember to be conscious of budget balance between partners when doing this). This workday allocation is expressed in what we call person months—PM—(or a percentage of a person month) and through this PM allocation, you calculate the budget for each partner in relation to how many PMs they have within the particular WP per task. Days within a PM have a fixed cost that you use to make this allocation of resources to each partner (see Fig. 3.10)

The following tables illustrate an example of labour budgeting:

The next step is the calculation of the average labour costs (see Fig. 3.11 for an example). The easiest way to do this is to develop one common calculation table that allows you to list the cost categories according to Call specific demands either per group or as a common average.

| IO1: Data research, analysis, implementation | 2 | 2,7 | 4,65 | 1,65 | 2,8 | 2,65 | 2,3 | 16,75 |
|---|---|---|---|---|---|---|---|---|
| Comparison and definition of processes including all relevant process parameters and collection of the data | 1 | 0,25 | 0,15 | 0,15 | 0,15 | 0,15 | 0,15 | 1,00 |
| Data analysis to assess performance, efficiency and sustainability of the processes | 4 | 0,85 | 0,75 | 0,75 | 1,5 | 1 | 1 | 5,85 |
| Problem identification based on the analysis | 2 | 0,85 | 1,25 | 0,45 | 0,85 | 0,7 | 0,35 | 4,45 |
| Solution development based on the results and provision of the data for the learning platform | 2 | 0,55 | 2 | 0,15 | 0,15 | 0,65 | 0,65 | 4,15 |
| Generating WP Summery Report as a basis for running the Quality Gate and QG workshop | 2 | 0,2 | 0,5 | 0,15 | 0,15 | 0,15 | 0,15 | 1,30 |
| Other costs for this WP (Statistical calculstion) | | | 2.000 | | | | | 2.000 |
| WP Labour Costs | | 9.180 | 21.390 | 7.920 | 17.360 | 5.300 | 3.335 | 64.485 |
| WP accumulated costs | | 9.180 | 23.390 | 7.920 | 17.360 | 5.300 | 3.335 | 66.485 |

**Fig. 3.10** Effort planning

| Project Labour Calculation | | | | | | | | | |
|---|---|---|---|---|---|---|---|---|---|
| Name | Position | Hours per year | Yearly Salary | Pay Related Social Insurance | Total Salary Costs | Full Head Equivalent | normalised Cost/mon | Involvement in Project | |
| AAA | Senior Manager/Chair | 1.752 | 108.000,00 | 17.280,00 | 125.280,00 | 1,00 | 10.440,00 | 10% | 1.044,00 |
| BBB | Manager/Senior Res. | 1.752 | 63.500,00 | 10.160,00 | 73.660,00 | 1,00 | 6.138,33 | 40% | 2.455,33 |
| CCC | Junior Reseracher | 1.168 | 45.600,00 | 7.296,00 | 52.896,00 | 0,67 | 6.612,00 | 40% | 2.644,80 |
| DDD | Admin Support | 876 | 27.800,00 | 4.448,00 | 32.248,00 | 0,50 | 5.374,67 | 10% | 537,47 |
| | | | | Virtual Project Employee per normalised person-month | | | | 100% | 6.681,60 |

**Fig. 3.11** Labour cost calculation

Since some Calls request that the labour budget be expressed in person-days whilst others request a monthly basis it is easiest to use the format shown in Figs. 3.11 and 3.12 and then just use the days or monthly average as requested for the specific proposal.

Once you have calculated labour costs and transferred the average labour costs to your budget planning table, the XLS (the file extension in Microsoft Excel) will automatically generate a full project calculation. You can then see where or what to amend to meet the suggested funding limits.

When calculating the overall budget, do not forget non-labour costs (see Fig. 3.13). Your non-labour related costs account for expenses directly associated with the project's implementation, such as equipment, travel, and subcontracting services (*direct costs*). Be specific and realistic in estimating these costs, and ensure they align with the funding programme's guidelines and restrictions. In some programmes there are fixed rates for all travel related costs, such as airfares, mileage, accommodation, and subsistence that depend on the travel distance and venue of meeting.

Many EU programmes allow for *indirect costs*. These incorporate overhead costs, such as organisational administration, rent, and utilities, which support the project but are not directly attributable to specific activities. Most EU funding programmes have a fixed percentage for indirect costs, so ensure you adhere to the guidelines provided.

Please keep in mind that all costs listed (both direct and indirect) require justification, for example, direct costs such as employment contracts or salary rates (though rates for labour are often set by the EU for different grades—researcher, technician, etc.) for the persons involved that justify the labour costs claimed or an indirect cost such as overheads. Clearly explain the relevance of these costs to the project's objectives and activities within the application. This ensures transparency and demonstrates your project's cost-effectiveness and efficient use of resources.

| | WP 0 | WP 1 | WP 2 | WP 3 | WP 4 | WP 5 | |
|---|---|---|---|---|---|---|---|
| P1 | 4,00 | 6,50 | 7,00 | 17,00 | 10,00 | 9,50 | 54,00 |
| P2 | 1,50 | 8,00 | 1,50 | 1,50 | 1,00 | 3,50 | 17,00 |
| P3 | 0,00 | 1,00 | 1,00 | 0,00 | 2,00 | 1,00 | 5,00 |
| | 5,50 | 15,50 | 9,50 | 18,50 | 13,00 | 14,00 | 76,00 |

**Fig. 3.12** Efforts per partner and WP for transfer to overview tables on the portal

| | | | | | | |
|---|---|---|---|---|---|---|
| PM | 6,3 | 2,0 | 3,7 | 1,9 | 1,5 | 15 |
| Euro/PM | 7.500 | 6.600 | 8.000 | 3.500 | 2.100 | |
| Normalised Man-Hour | 53,6 | 47,1 | 57,1 | 25,0 | 15,0 | |
| Personnel | 46.875 | 12.870 | 29.200 | 6.650 | 3.045 | 98.640 |
| Subcontracting | 8.000 | 2.000 | 2.000 | 2.000 | 2.000 | 16.000 |
| Other Direct Costs | 10.200 | 9.950 | 8.400 | 10.950 | 4.400 | 43.900 |
| Indirect Costs | 34.245 | 13.692 | 7.520 | 3.520 | 1.489 | 60.466 |
| Lump Sum | | | | | | |
| TOTAL: | 99.320 | 38.512 | 47.120 | 23.120 | 10.934 | 219.006 |
| Official Overhead Rate | 60% | 60% | 20% | 20% | 20% | |

**Fig. 3.13** Cost types besides labour

As we have previously highlighted an important issue when calculating, your budget is the balance between partners and regions. Regional distribution has a political dimension in that no one region can be more favoured than another in the funding distribution. As a rule of thumb, you can say that in a multi-regional proposal with upwards of four regions represented, no region should receive more than 1/3 of the total budget. The project coordinator (usually you as you have initiated and written the project proposal) should always represent the biggest individual budget allocation. The only exception to this is in the case of a task leader within a WP. In these cases, the lead organisation within a WP receives more resources than any other partner involved reflecting their WP management role.

Salary rates for roles such as research assistant within your application are not based on a standardised EU costing. The EU requires that you calculate these rates according to the average salary scale for the role within the country where the proposed research or patriating academic, such as a professor, is located. This means salaries allocation can vary very widely between partners and therefore have implications for the overall budget distribution between your consortium partners.

Thus, it might be that one partner comes from a low-cost salary region and another partner from a high-salary region. That difference can go up to a ratio of 1:4.

In these cases, it is advisable for you to incorporate into your resource distribution planning these regional salary differentials and their implications for your overall budget when deciding who to approach to join your consortium.

You need to avoid the error of balancing the project budget by increasing the labour effort of low-cost regions by just giving them more person-days for a similar task compared to a partner from a high-cost region. The evaluators will immediately recognise this and lower the score of the project based on bad resource planning. However, if you have such a differential between partners doing the same task, you must explain the reasons for it.

If you have real cause to use a partner from a low-cost region for a specific job to keep the overall project budget efficient, then please say so. You need to argue that due to the relative cost differences between different partners, combined with their expertise, the workload balance was intentionally shifted to the lower cost partner to provide a cost-efficient use of project resources. Then you can have an exception where that partner might in total have more person-days involved in the project than the coordinating partner for a particular work package.

Not all programmes award 100% of a project's costs. Some only finance between 50% and 80% of the total costs. In such cases, you are required to make up the difference through a contribution from your organisation's resources, commonly called *match funding*.

In most cases match funding consists of a calculation of programme unfunded labour (that is the work of you and your partners) that you will do on the project which will be funded by your organisation through your normal salary. Generally, your organisation will not want to incur real costs in relation to a project. Therefore, in reality you and your partners will be taking on extra work in addition to your normal day-to-day duties for your organisation. You should check that all individuals within your consortium understand this should it arise.

Should you win funding, a percentage of the total grant will be held back by the EU funders. The balance is paid once the project is evaluated as meeting its stated goals. This means in reality that your organisation will incur some costs as the project proceeds and will then be reimbursed these costs once the project is completed (usually two to three months post receipt by the EU of your project's completion report).

Also remember, if the EU programme evaluators are not satisfied with the outcomes of your project, they can either withhold the balance of the grant or demand reimbursement from you and your partners' organisations of the entire grant. Figure 3.14 graph indicates the cost and cash flow with a simplified example.

Having drafted these allocations, you then need to ask your partners to check how realistic the allocation is per task from their perspective. This can be a very involved discussion and you need to ensure you do not leave it until the last minute in relation to the submission deadline.

You also need to make clear to partners that this is a DRAFT exercise and will be subject to changes prior to submission as PMs may have to be readjusted to make sure an overall budget balance is achieved between partners (you will of course inform them of such changes should they arise) in relation to the application.

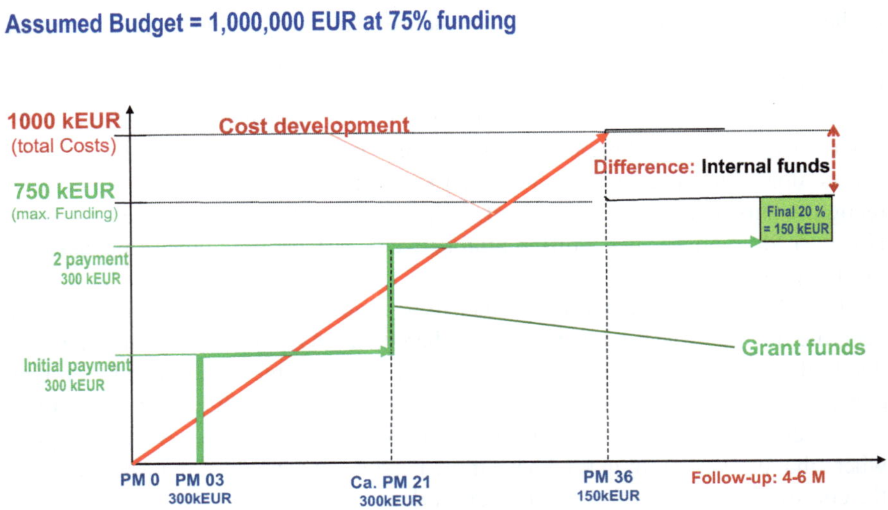


**Fig. 3.14** Cash flow in an EU project

### *3.4.2 Mandates*

Once you have defined the budget, and through your work packages and task distribution, you then need to obtain what are called mandates from all partners. Obtaining mandates from project partners confirms their commitment and authorisation to participate in the project (a mandate is a document—the format of which is standardised for all partners—that is a signed commitment by the recognised legal representative of a participant organisation).

Obtaining mandates is a requirement of many programmes, ensuring that all partners are committed to the project's success, reinforcing the credibility and viability of your application in the eyes of evaluators.

In summary, accurately calculating budgets and obtaining mandates from project partners are essential aspects of crafting a successful application for EU-funded projects. By paying close attention to these elements ensuring transparency, alignment, and commitment of all partners involved.

## 3.5 Managing the EU Submission Portal

As we said in Chap. 2 (Sect. 2.5) the EU has established a Funding and Tenders Opportunities Portal. This is now the single entry point for finding and managing EU grants. However, you submit your application through a specific programme online portal. Unfortunately, there is no standardised application form portal, but rather a wide range of EU submission portals. For example, the EU4Health portal, the ERASMUS+ portal, and the Horizon portal, whilst sharing some common features, are also different from one another.

Submission portals are also subject to change from year-to-year so never assume that because you have submitted through a specific EU programme Call portal in the past, that particular portal will be the same for your latest application.

Below are some tips for you when dealing with an EU grant portal:

- **Read the guidelines:** Read the call text and its requirements. This will ensure you are meeting all the requirements in all sections of the application on the portal site.
- **Agree on limiting those who can directly interact with the online application form on the portal**: Whilst you may want partners in your consortium to write some sections of the application, to do this transfer the online application form to a shared MS Word document and collaboratively work on that rather than directly working on the online application form. After you have written the narrative on your MS Word document then "cut and paste" the content into the appropriate section within the online application form.
- Ensure there is no more than one (usually you) or two individuals from your consortium who will act as overall editor and who have the sole responsibility for the transfer of the Word document into the online application form to minimise confusion and make errors less likely; as the old English adage goes "too many cooks spoil the broth!"
- **Save regularly**: Many platforms have glitches, freeze/"go down". Therefore, it is wise to save your input on to the online application form regularly to minimise any loss of input. It is difficult enough to do the work once but twice, three, or four times, particularly when under time constraints, can be very demoralising!
- **Start early**: At busy times (for example, around the submission deadline), the portal system may start "glitching" due to extra demands placed upon it by the sheer number of applicants trying to access it. This can risk you not being able to submit your application. Some of us have had the experience of failing to submit because we had only five minutes left before the portal closed to submissions per the deadline and we could not upload the application because the "traffic" was so heavy.
- Such an event can be deeply distressing bearing in mind how hard you have worked on your application. It can also be humiliating when explaining such a failure to your partners. **Therefore, the earlier you can submit, the better, to avoid stress.**
- **Experiment with the portal**: Before you start the official process, experiment with a dummy account to see what steps are needed, etc. The earlier you understand the system, the better.
- **Validate (if possible):** Some portals allow you to do what is termed "validating" your application. By pressing this button, the portal highlights missing information that is required to make a successful application. It is a very useful function.
- **Pay attention to extra requirements:** The proposal is often one piece of the application. Most grant programmes require substantial data gathered from

partners (for example, 5 relevant publications/projects). You may have to submit other sections such as a draft data management plan and/or complete or submit an ethics section. Be alert to check for these as they can be very involved.

- **Ethics:** If there is a requirement to fill in an ethics section within the application, do NOT leave this to the last moment. Ethical issues and addressing them can be complex and it surprises us how often such a complex aspect of the application (and from an EU evaluator's point view a very important element) is left to the last minute. As a result, the quality of the ethics narrative can be poor and you will be penalised by evaluators as a result.
- **Review:** Ensure that you give yourself time to review the different elements of the application—particularly when you need to cross-reference what you write with the specific content to be found in the Call document. In addition, it can be difficult to recognise inconsistencies, lack of clarity, omissions, or errors when you are regularly reading the same materials. It may be helpful to get the fresh eyes of a colleague or partner also to review your narrative content.
- **Getting support to dealing with portal problems**: You may run into issues and questions when using the portal. You can ask your NCP for help or what is called, "raise tickets" within the system. These alert the portal administrators in Brussels that you have encountered a problem with which you need help. Whilst the portal administrators will contact you, there can be a delay. Unless there is a complete system failure (which is not unknown) you will not receive a deadline extension in relation to portal problems, so the earlier you raise a ticket the better!

### *3.5.1 The Online Submission*

The final step in the online application is the submission. The submission is through the online portal associated with the specific programme call. The portal submission process can be challenging, even for those familiar with the process. This section therefore describes the process of submission. It also deals with challenges that can arise and how to manage them.

The EU grant submission is notorious amongst researchers for technical challenges, especially when there is a lot of traffic. Therefore, try to submit your application through the portal as soon as possible and well in advance of the deadline when most people will be using it and it has the highest chances of crashing. We acknowledge that this is often easier said than done! Nevertheless, as a matter of operating principle, you should try.

#### Partner Details

As soon as you can, find out what information will be required from partners. Firstly, you will need their Participant Identification Code (PIC) and/or Organisation ID (OID). These are unique numbers attached to organisations who wish to apply/

participate in EU-funded programmes. An organisation cannot participate in an application without a PIC and or OID.

Most organisations within the EU who have previously participated in funded programmes will have one. If one of your partners has not previously participated in an EU Call, they will need to apply for a PIC/ OID through the portal and a code will be allocated to them. Note this is not an immediate allocation and can take some time. Therefore, make sure that you check the PIC/OID status of your partners right at the beginning of your project.

In addition to the above, also check the PIC/OID status of partners who have previously participated and that their PIC/OID status is up-to-date. Partner organisations who have previously participated in many EU projects can, over time, acquire a number of PICs (for example, associated with research institutions within the participating organisation) and these will all be listed—make sure you enter onto the portal the most up-to-date one and the specific PIC associated with your partner.

Subsequently you may need to add a range of detailed information about partner organisations. This includes subdivisions of legal entities, units, addresses, email addresses, and telephone numbers. You may also need to add information about individuals attached to an application including title (for example, "Prof." versus "Dr."), name, position, gender, career stage (for example, early career) and/or ORCID ID.

You can highlight key partner publications, projects, or datasets pertinent to the subject matter of the Call. These serve to highlight the capacity and suitability of the project partners for the project. The fields can often be filled in by partners directly, but you may be able to fill in these details yourself; not filling them in would be missed opportunity to emphasise your consortium's expertise and project capacity!

## Main Proposal Text and Appendixes

Ensure that the main proposal text is in the right format (for example, word or pdf) and is formatted as outlined in the guidelines (for example, page numbers, font, font size, spacing, alignment, etc.). The text should be easy to read and aims, objectives, work plan, etc. should be clear for the evaluator! Text outside the recommended page numbers/character limit will be considered. Consider if you need to include a reference list in the main body or whether you can submit references as an Appendix.

Check your main body narrative for grammar, spelling errors, and missing text. Also, check that wherever you refer to the title of your proposal in the narrative it is consistent. Because a proposal title can go through a number of iterations/changes, the title can be mis-written in the narrative and not be consistent with the title used to head your application. Check that all sections are fully complete and that questions asked within the application form are answered fully. Delete any pages that may need to be deleted. Ensure that no comments or suggested edits or track changes remain on the application.

Check whether you are required to submit appendices such as data management plans or ethical reviews. You can use Open AIRE's Argos Tool to generate data management plans (https://argos.openaire.eu/home). Some public data management plans can be found here (https://argos.openaire.eu/explore-plans).

Be cognizant of requirements related to making data your project generates open access/source and FAIR (Findable, Accessible, Interoperable and Reusable). As we said earlier, all data should be, "as open as possible, as closed as necessary". There may be a template and guidelines that you can use to fill in the ethical review documents.

Check requirements in relation to your budget. For example, when submitting application in response to an EU4Health Call, we found that in addition to submitting budget details within the main application form, we were also required to input such data into a series of appendices. We had failed to notice this requirement initially and as a result were placed under considerable stress in the latter part of submitting the application through the portal.

## 3.6 Conclusion

Writing a clear and accessible application clearly referenced to EU and Call policy priorities underpinned by an established strong consortium partnership is crucial for making a successful application for funding. Clarity of narrative is key to making a convincing case that your project is worth funding. Pay close attention to the precision of the language used in your submission. Remember that English for many evaluators is their second language so choose simple plain language instead of overly complex and technical language.

You have to convince the evaluators that your proposal is strongly aligned with the Call objectives and that it will deliver innovative sustainable impacts beyond the funded lifetime of the project. The evaluators will want to see this reflected in a realistic methodology that will deliver on what you promise (remember not to over promise on what you can deliver). A well-explained and realistic budget allocation goes a long way to convince an evaluator of this.

In conclusion, despite your best efforts and a well-prepared application, there is always a degree of uncertainty involved in the EU submission process. If your application is not selected for funding, you need to re-evaluate your approach and perhaps seek an alternative funding source. One of the positive aspects of engaging with EU funding calls is that you will always receive feedback on why your proposal was not funded which can then use to hone your idea/application for future funding calls.

**C.-Andreas Dalluege** Founder and Managing Partner of IBK Group; Chairman of the European Business Excellence Network e.V.; National Council Member of the Irish Work Study Institute. Certified Advisor & Trainer of EFQM, Operating Partner and Trainer of Initiative Ludwig-Erhard-Preis (ILEP).

Since 1990 he participated as the senior researcher for his organisation in over 35 EU projects in most programme types offered by the EU and represented his company in all of them at the Management Board level as well as worked as our lead researcher in them.

He serves on the national board of the Irish Work Study Institute (IIESMS) and as President of the European Business Excellence Network (EuroBEN).

As a lecturer at the TH Aschaffenburg, he also gives classes on the design, proposing, and running of EU Research projects since 2019. Contact: cad@ibk.eu

**Florian Scheibein** is a Research Assistant and PhD student at the School of Health Sciences, South East Technological University. He is currently the Lead Research Assistant for an EU4Health project—DDS-MAP—and Grant Holder Manager for an EU COST Action—CUPID. He has been involved in three ERASMUS projects and was the co-recipient of the Council of Europe Pompidou Group European Drug Prevention Prize for one of these projects. He is an Editor for the Harm Reduction Journal and is a Co-Director and General Secretary of the Network of Early Career Professionals in Addiction Medicine which works with the World Health Organisation's Alcohol, Drugs, and Addictive Behaviours Unit. Contact: Florian.Scheibein@setu.ie

**Gregor Štiglic** Professor and head of the Research Institute at the University of Maribor, Faculty of Health Sciences. Since 2014, he has served as Vice Dean for Research at the same faculty, where he coordinates the research work of various research groups. He has led and worked on numerous research projects in digital healthcare and application of advanced artificial intelligence methods in healthcare.

In the past decade, he has served as a reviewer and panel member for different funding agencies such as EU Horizon Europe, UKRI Medical Research Council, The Netherlands Organisation for Scientific Research—NWO and The Research Council of Norway. Contact: gregor.stiglic@um.si

**John Stephen Gary Wells** PhD, FAAN, FNMFRCSI (Ad Eundem) is Dean of the School of Health Sciences at the South East Technological University. John graduated from the University of Manchester with a degree in history. Following graduation, he trained and practised as a mental health nurse in London, eventually managing one of the busiest acute psychiatric admission units in the capital. John then transitioned from a clinical practice role to an academic one in 1993, moving to Ireland in 1998 to take up an academic position there.

John is an active and experienced researcher. As either Principal Investigator or co-investigator he has won funding from national and EU-funded research programmes to the value of 12 million Euros. He is a member of the National Research Ethics Committee for Clinical Trials in Ireland and holds visiting professorships at UCD, Ireland, King's College London, UK, and Maribor University, Slovenia. John has published 115 peer-reviewed papers, 7 technical reports (commissioned by regional, national, and EU agencies), 9 book chapters, and 1 book.

At the time of publication he is principal investigator for an EU4Health-funded project on enhancing the digital skills of the pan-European health care workforce. He is also chairperson of a COST Action on expanding the access of people with intellectual disabilities to cancer services. Contact: john.wells@setu.ie

# Chapter 4
# Notification of Outcome and Contracts

**C.-Andreas Dalluege, Aleksandra Lovrenčič, and Florian Scheibein**

This chapter deals with the inter-related subjects of notification of outcome and contracts. Often, after you receive a notification that your application has been successful, the funder will require post-funding amendments to your original application.

## 4.1 Notification of Outcome

The notification of outcome is an eagerly anticipated moment. Sometimes it can take six months or longer to receive a notification of an application outcome. A notification contains (1) an evaluation scored summary report and (2) a funding decision.

**The Evaluation Summary Report (ESR)**: The ESR details the evaluator's assessment of your proposal compared to the funding criteria in terms of a score and narrative explanation focusing on strengths and weaknesses of your application. A minimum threshold score (for example, 15/20 is usually applied) in relation to the degree to which a project could be funded.

C.-A. Dalluege (✉)
IBK, Wiesbaden, Germany
e-mail: cad@ibk.eu

A. Lovrenčič
University Maribor, Maribor, Slovenia
e-mail: aleksandra.lovrencic@um.si

F. Scheibein
South East Technological University, Waterford, Ireland
e-mail: Florian.Scheibein@setu.ie



C.-A. Dalluege, J. S. G. Wells (eds.), *Navigating an EU Research Project*, Management for Professionals, https://doi.org/10.1007/978-3-031-70928-9_4

Crossing the minimum score threshold does not necessarily guarantee funding. Because within any call there are limited funds, applications that cross the funding threshold are ordered in terms of their score. Those with the highest score beyond the threshold will be funded.

There are several types of funding decision. The first, and most common, is a rejection where the minimum threshold has not been achieved. Secondly, a rejection where the minimum threshold has been achieved but where the application is not placed on a reserve list. A third decision is where the minimum threshold has been achieved or exceeded and the project has been placed on a reserve list pending potential further funding. Finally, the most desirable decision is a notification that your proposal will be funded.

If your project is successful, you will receive further advice on the next steps you need to pursue administratively. Typically, this involves finalising a Grant Agreement, budget, work plan and consortium agreement. In some cases, you may be asked to review and adjust various aspects of the proposal such as deliverables and milestones and you may be asked to include key performance indicators required by the funder. For example, in our recently EU4Health-funded project (DDS-MAP) we were asked to adjust some deliverables and include extra measures to validate its outcomes.

## 4.2 Types of Contracts

The contract defines the roles, responsibilities and obligations of all parties (EU funders and consortium partners) involved in the project. Understanding the types of contracts is essential to ensure effective project implementation and management within the context of EU-funded projects.

- **The Grant Agreement**: The contract between the EU funder and the consortium is usually called The Grant Agreement. This agreement forms the foundation of the project by outlining the rights and obligations of the funder and the consortium. It covers aspects such as project objectives, work plans, budgets reporting requirements and other terms and conditions. It can also address ownership issues related to intellectual property rights (IPR). The Grant Agreement is signed by the project co-ordinator on behalf of the consortium. However, sometimes all partner organisations are required to sign this contract.
- **The Consortium Agreement:** The Consortium Agreement is a binding contract signed between all the consortium partners involved in the project. This can be a voluntary contracting process or is required by the EU funders as a condition of funding. It outlines partners' roles, responsibilities and contributions, towards the project's success.
- Typically, the Consortium Agreement should cover decision-making processes, conflict resolution procedures, intellectual property rights and how funds will be allocated.

- **Subcontracts**: Subcontracts are agreements made between project partners and external entities such as consultants or service providers who contribute their expertise or services to the project. It is essential to manage these subcontracts to ensure that they align with the project's objectives, budget, timeline and comply with EU procurement regulations. Generally speaking, the prospect of subcontracting should be outlined in your proposal when making your application. However, sometimes an unforeseen issue arises which necessitates a subcontract. In these circumstances, permission must be sought from the EU prior to entering a subcontract with an external party.
- For example, in one of our previous projects (ROSE), a project partner lost a skill-set—language translation (due to a team member leaving) that could not be replaced from within the consortium—leading to the need for a reallocation of budget to a translation subcontractor for which permission from the EU was granted.
- **Intellectual Property (IP) Agreements**: IP contracts govern the ownership, usage and dissemination of any property generated during the project. This can include patents, copyrights, trademarks or other forms of property.
- IP agreements play a role, in defining ownership rights, licensing arrangements and any restrictions related to using or sharing the results of a project. It is important to remember that as a general rule, the results of a project funded by the EU should be made generally available free of such restrictions. Therefore, IP agreements are becoming less of a feature within EU-funded projects. As we indicated in Chap. 3, should intellectual property rights be a feature of your project, this needs to be made explicit in your application.
- **Confidentiality agreements**: Related to IP agreements are confidentiality agreements—sometimes called non-disclosure agreements (NDAs). These are legal contracts created to protect sensitive or proprietary information exchanged between partners involved in a project. These agreements outline which information must be kept confidential. They specify the duration of confidentiality and include any exceptions or obligations related to the agreement. Again, you should remember that the EU commitment to open access to information means that you should outline and justify these within your application for funding.
- **Data sharing agreements**: These govern the sharing, storage and use of data generated or collected throughout a project. These agreements cover aspects such as data protection, privacy measures, access rights and data retention policies. It is essential for these agreements to comply with data protection regulations like the General Data Protection Regulation (GDPR).
- **Employment contracts**: These are agreements between project partners and individuals hired for project work (such as a research assistant). They detail terms and conditions related to employment including roles and responsibilities, salary details, benefits offered, contract duration and termination. It is important for these contracts to adhere to local labour laws and regulations.

## 4.3 Finalising Contracts and Getting Them Signed

Receiving the contract and ensuring it is properly signed is a milestone in securing EU funding for your project. The contract serves as an agreement between your consortium and the funding agency outlining elements such as project goals, activities, timeline, budget and more.

Negotiating a contract can take time ranging from weeks to months, depending on the complexity of the project and the number of issues that arise. It is crucial to remain patient and persistent throughout this process while keeping in mind that your ultimate goal is to secure a contract that benefits both your consortium and the funding agency.

In this section, we outline the steps involved in obtaining and finalising the contract, including negotiation, legal review and reaching an understanding.

- **Negotiating the contract**: Once your project proposal receives approval for funding the next step involves negotiating the terms of the contract with the funding agency. This process includes a series of discussions and exchanges between your project consortium and the contracting authority to finalise all aspects of the project and come to an agreement on terms.
- **Points of negotiation**: During this negotiation process key factors that may be subject to discussion include project objectives, activities, timeline requirements for budget allocation, intellectual property rights, consortium structure, reporting requirements, intellectual property rights and other relevant elements. It's crucial to be well prepared in providing information or clarifying any aspects as needed during these negotiations.
- **Communication**: Maintaining communication, with the funding agency throughout this negotiation phase is vital. It is also extremely important to keep all project partners informed about discussions and any changes regarding the project details so that they agree as the negotiation proceeds.
- **Reviewing the draft contract**: Before signing the contract, it is necessary to conduct a review. This step ensures that the agreement complies with all laws, regulations, guidelines and protects the interests of your project consortium.
- When reviewing the contract, you should engage with experts who specialise in EU-funding contracts—often based in your organisation's research support unit or legal department. They will carefully examine every aspect of the agreement and provide guidance on any concerns, risks or issues needing clarification before signing.
- **Finalising the contract**: Once the negotiation and legal review processes are complete, the last step is to finalise the contract. This involves incorporating any agreed-upon changes or amendments into the document that accurately reflect the understanding of project details and terms by both the consortium and funding agency.
- You and your partners will need to identify from within your organisation who is the recognised legal representative to sign the finalised contract. Usually, this same person signed the project mandate during the submission process.

- Coordinating the signature process is crucial to ensure that all required parties sign in an order and within specified timeframes. The signing procedure may involve in-person signatures, mailing of documents or using portals based on preferences and requirements set by the funding agency. Remember to keep copies of signed contracts for record-keeping purposes and distribute them to all project partners and stakeholders involved.
- After a contract is signed, there may be other steps that need to be taken before officially commencing your project. This includes developing and signing a Consortium Agreement that outlines roles, responsibilities, relationships among project partners while aligning with the terms stated in the EU-funding contract. The Consortium Agreement should cover aspects such as resource allocation, decision-making processes, dispute resolution mechanisms, addressing intellectual property rights.
- **Monitoring the contract:** To ensure progress is monitored effectively throughout the duration of the project it is essential to establish a framework for monitoring and evaluation. This framework will help you assess impact and track progress according to reporting requirements specified in the contract. Moreover, it will allow you to identify areas that may need improvement along the way.
- Depending on what sub-contracted services are provided in relation to the contract specific timelines for each payment will be established. In some cases, subcontractors may also be required to submit progress reports, alongside their invoices. These reports provide an overview of the completed work that justifies payment. They include a list of all the deliverables submitted as any challenges faced and potential delays.

In summary securing and finalising a contract for an EU-funded project involves steps such as negotiation, legal examination and finalisation.

## 4.4 Amendments and Changes to Existing Contracts

As we indicated in relation to subcontracting, sometimes during a project's execution there might be a need to modify or amend existing contracts due to changes, in circumstances, scope or objectives. Such amendments between partners need mutual agreement between the partners concerned and co-ordinator and documented formally to ensure compliance with requirements and prevent disputes.

It is important to note that the EU-funding agency will only permit such changes in situations where the reasons are beyond the control of the project consortium. For instance, due to the COVID lockdown, an extension to the SSTeMM project was sought at no extra cost to the budget. This was granted (it should be noted that later on the EU-funding agency also agreed to additional funding as the lockdown continued). Below we deal in more detail with some of these issues of amendment.

## 4.5 Amending Work Plan and Budget

Changes to work plans and budget amendments sometimes are requested by the EU following initial approval. This can occur for a range of reasons. For example, the funding agency may disapprove of subcontracting arrangement and require that such work be allocated to one or more consortium partners. Alternatively, there may be differing requirements specific to a grant programme, specific sections (for example, gender or open science) that have been tightened up since the call was issued or certain pieces of work may need to be removed due to funding restrictions.

Some things to consider before changing the work plan/budget

- Assess the impact: Small changes can have big impacts in terms of the progress of your project's objectives, activities, timeline, resources and overall feasibility. Potential risks and benefits should be considered and discussed with project partners, stakeholders and the funding agencies
- Seeking approval: As we indicated earlier, if you need change in budget allocation you will need to get approval from the funding agency and/or consortium or both before making such changes
- Review grant agreement and consortium agreement: consider are there any aspects within these agreements that need to be changed and, if so, how could you initiate such change.

## 4.6 Budget Issues to Monitor Over the Course of Your Project

- **Equipment**: Equipment budgets are governed by EU regulations that consider national differential depreciation rates over the lifetime of a project. This means that if two partners from different countries purchased the same equipment within their respective jurisdictions, funding amounts may vary, based on how depreciation of such equipment is calculated within their respective countries. For example, two partners buy equipment of the same type in their respective jurisdictions for use in a project over its lifetime. In one country the national rules may state that the depreciation period is three years for this type of equipment, whilst in the other country its national rules may state seven years. As a result, the first partner would be eligible for 2/3 of its equipment depreciation cost as expenses while the second partner would only receive 2/7 depreciation cost as expenses.
- **Subsistence and travel**: Subsistence reimbursements are determined based on the expenses incurred up to certain limits. Some programmes offer fixed amounts, for categories of travel expenses (such as transportation, accommodation and meals), whilst others focus on how much you spend within limits.
- Travel expenses raise concerns due to project travel cost regulations associated with each programme. Some programmes have defined "quality limits" when it

comes to things like economy flights or accommodation. You should note that due to environmental concerns, the EU increasingly prefers partners to use public transport, particularly trains, for travel to partner countries rather than planes. Therefore, make sure you justify clearly face-to-face meetings which involve international travel where flights are costed as opposed to trains.

- **Subcontracting:** Subcontracting is another cost category that requires consideration and evaluation if you plan to utilise it. The EU general view is that if a specific expertise is necessary then this should be within the consortium partners. Subcontracting is only acceptable for short-term activities that would be costly within the consortium or arise due to an unforeseen circumstance, such as losing key personnel, as we outlined earlier. Examples of subcontracting activities could include obtaining translation services for conferences or renting exhibition booths at trade shows or external conferences.
- **Indirect costs**: Indirect costs may involve office and utility expenses. Typically, indirect costs are calculated as a percentage of the project's costs based on the funding agency's guidelines. In EU-funded projects these indirect costs are allocated as a fixed percentage of your budget without requiring justification.

## 4.7 Reporting Costs and Activities Over the Project's Trajectory

It is important to document and justify expenses in line with the rules and guidelines of the funding agency. EU-funded projects necessitate reporting at defined points (usually interim and end-point reporting) to demonstrate compliance with assigned budgets. These reports involve creating and submitting statements that provide an overview of project expenses and financial performance.

Most programmes require reporting labour costs through partners providing a time-sheet for each person involved in the project in relation to the hours they worked on each task for each work package (see Fig. 4.1). Remaining cost details are provided within a defined table format.

Figures 4.1 and 4.2 provide examples of time-sheet reporting that we have used in our projects. Partners need to complete fields such as "Activities Performed", "Results Achieved" and "Person Days" while other information is already included in the template provided. Each partner sends this data to the project co-ordinator who compiles these into an overall consortium Quarterly Summary report (Fig. 4.2). These are combined to form the basis of the interim and final reports that are sent to the EU-funding agency.

For clarity in reporting, particularly as a lump sum grant is now generally the standard funding allocation (there are some exceptions such as coordination and support actions (CSA) in HORIZON) used by the EU it is important to include monthly and quarterly cost reporting, at the work package level (this will help you to keep an oversight of costs). This includes fields for calculating costs per work

gefördert durch
Erasmus+

| | |
|---|---|
| **Time Sheet for 1st Project Quarter** | |
| **For:** | **C.-Andreas Dalluege** |
| **Period covered:** | **September 2019** |
| **Project:** | **SSTeMM** |
| **Agreement number:** | 2019-1-IE02-KA203-000663 |
| **Project number:** | 2019-1-IE02-KA203-000663 |
| **Institution:** | IBK Management Solutions GmbH |
| **Company Position:** | Managing Partner |
| **Work Contract:** | Employment contract of 7. Dec. 2001 |
| **Project Tasks:** | Manager & Researcher |

| Date / Period (dd/mm/yyyy) | Topic of Work | Task | Activities Performed | Results achieved | Person Days | Function in this task |
|---|---|---|---|---|---|---|
| 27+30.09.2019 | Design of a "work stress analysis" including digital transformation in the health care sector | 1.2 | Discussions with WIT to clarify issues within the IMPRESS SFA questionnaire for usage within SSTeMM | Clarification of issues regarding the SFA questionnaire | 0.50 | Researcher |
| 18.09.2019 | Quality Gate 1: Well-tested BRAINS Analytical Toolbox | 1.13 | Preparing a chapter explaining the Quality Gate process to be added to the Project Manual | QG Chapter added to PM | 1.00 | Researcher |
| | | | | | **1.50** | |
| | | | | | **1.50** | Research Tasks |
| | | | | | **0.00** | Technical Tasks |

**Fig. 4.1** Monthly time-sheet

package and month providing an overview of all costs related to a delivery (work package or intellectual output) when preparing reports (see Fig. 4.3).

## 4.8 Submitting Reports

Regularly reporting on the progress of the project to the EU-funding agency project office, project partners and other stakeholders is both an expectation in terms of formal reports—interim and final and good practice in relation to your consortium partners. Make sure that the reports are clear precise and delivered on time. These reports should highlight the accomplishments, difficulties and influence of the project.

For a typical three-year funded project, the interim report usually covers the first 18 months of activity and submission to the funding agency is due by the end of month 19. There may be some variations in dates based on specific calls and shorter or longer project length. The final report covers the remaining duration of the project. The deadline, for submission of this final report (covering the last 18 months of activity and overall results, is two months after the funded completion date of project activities.

In some cases, additional reports may be necessary; for example, if a project partner fails to fulfil their responsibilities and budget reallocation becomes necessary or if the project undergoes a random audit by the funders or EU court of auditors.

gefördert durch

Erasmus+

**Time Sheet for 1st Project Quarter**

| | |
|---|---|
| **For:** | **C.-Andreas Dalluege** |
| **Period covered:** | **1.09. 2019 - 30.11.2019** |
| **Project:** | **SSTeMM** |
| **Agreement number:** | 2019-1-IE02-KA203-000663 |
| **Project number:** | 2019-1-IE02-KA203-000663 |
| **Institution:** | IBK Management Solutions GmbH |
| **Company Position:** | Managing Partner |
| **Work Contract:** | Employment contract of 7. Dec. 2001 |
| **Project Tasks:** | Manager & Researcher |

**Overview C.-Andreas Dalluege - PQ1**

| Period | Manager | Researcher /Trainer | Technical | Amin | in total |
|---|---|---|---|---|---|
| September 2019 | n.a. | 1.50 | 0.00 | n.a. | 1.50 |
| October 2019 | n.a. | 2.00 | 0.00 | n.a. | 2.00 |
| November 2019 | n.a. | 2.00 | 0.00 | n.a. | 2.00 |
| Total | **0.00** | **5.50** | **0.00** | **0.00** | **5.50** |

**05/12/19**
Date | Signature (employee)

**05/12/19**
Date | Signature (employer)

**Fig. 4.2** Quarterly time-sheet summary

When preparing reports, you, as project co-ordinator, will receive a template from the funding agency. It is crucial to use this specific document to organise your reports because minor details may vary from one reporting period to another. Not using the provided template could potentially result in a rejection of the report by the funding agency. Most reporting is through an online portal and report template so it is unlikely that you will have the opportunity to provide your own bespoke template!

Cofinanciado por la Unión Europea

**Time Sheet for 1st Project Quarter**

| | |
|---|---|
| **For:** | **C.-Andreas Dalluege** |
| **Period covered:** | **December 2022** |
| **Project:** | **ExCurS** |
| **Project number:** | 2022-1-ES01-KA220-VET-000086786 |
| **Institution:** | IBK Management Solutions GmbH |
| **Company Position:** | Managing Partner |
| **Work Contract:** | Employment contract of 2002 with addendum 2022 |
| **Project Tasks:** | Manager & Researcher |
| **Daily rate** | 323,04 € |

**WP1 Project & Quality Management**

| Date / Period (dd/mm/yyyy) | Task name | Task No. | Activities Performed | Results achieved | Person days | Cost |
|---|---|---|---|---|---|---|
| 19-22.-12. | Establish Project Steering and Management Group and publish the Project Manual (PM) | 1.2 | Cooperating withh GAIA to prepare and run the Project Kick-off Meeting | Project Kick-off Meeting run on 22.12. | 1,00 | 323,04 |
| | | | | | 1,00 | 323,04 |

**WP2 IO1: ExCurS Concept & Self-Assessment Support**

| Date / Period (dd/mm/yyyy) | Task name | Task No. | Activities Performed | Results achieved | Person days | Cost |
|---|---|---|---|---|---|---|
| | | | None yet | | 0,00 | 0,00 |
| | | | | | 0,00 | 0,00 |

**WP5 Project Dissemination, Exploitation and Impact**

| Date / Period (dd/mm/yyyy) | Task name | Task No. | Activities Performed | Results achieved | Person days | Cost |
|---|---|---|---|---|---|---|
| | | | None yet | | 0,00 | 0,00 |
| | | | | | 0,00 | 0,00 |

| Days | Cost | |
|---|---|---|
| 1,00 | 323,04 | WP1 |
| 0,00 | 0,00 | WP2 |
| | | WP3 |
| | | WP4 |
| 0,00 | 0,00 | WP5 |
| 1,00 | 323,04 | Montly Total |

These numbers will be transfered automatically to the Overview page

Date & signature of member of staff

Date, name & signature of the responsible of the organisation

**Fig. 4.3** Time-sheet for lump sum projects

You should note the reporting template is subject to change and may not be available for you to review at the start of your project, but near the reporting deadline. Therefore, we would recommend you create an "educated guess" template, based on previous templates for the particular funding programme, to organise your reporting information that you can adapt to the "new" reporting template when the EU project office of the particular programme gives you access.

It is crucial that you properly document all project expenses with supporting records, such as receipts, for each expenditure. These records might be necessary for verification purposes should you be audited. It's therefore crucial that you and your consortium partners keep all your documents organised and easily accessible in case the relevant agency wishes to review them.

This does not mean that you must send every expense related document to the funding agency, only send those that the agency requires or requests. The report template will offer guidance on documents you should retain and/or include with your report. In this regard, it would be practical to create a server space where you can store these documents in a manner and allow access during the evaluation period for results and finances.

## 4.9 Audit

Please bear in mind that projects funded by the European Union (EU) may undergo an audit. These are usually random so do not necessarily indicate that the funding agency has specific concerns about how you have used funds—though of course sometimes this is a reason for the audit.

Such an audit will carefully assess how the project is managed and its compliance with the rules and guidelines set by the funding agency. An audit can be conducted by either the funding agency itself external auditors, such as the Court of Auditors, or both.

In terms of avoiding a targeted audit (that is, one that is not based on a random project selection) it is essential to ensure that your financial reports are comprehensive, consistent and free from any issues that may trigger an audit. To achieve this, be proactive in identifying any risks or challenges that may arise and promptly report any issues to your allocated EU project officer.

Always report and seek permission for a budget reallocation within the project. Your EU Project Officer will acknowledge this communication and usually does not object so long as such reallocation is within the rules. If this communication doesn't occur, the financial audit office won't accept the change you made and may disallow the cost entirely. In turn, this may lead to a request for that amount not to be reimbursed and potentially prompt a full project audit.

During an audit your cooperation is expected by providing all requested information and documentation. It is crucial to review any findings from the audit and address any identified issues or discrepancies promptly by communicating with the auditors.

In some cases, you may be required to reimburse funding for cost items if they are determined not justifiable for project use. Remember that during audits it is not up to the EU to prove that you claimed costs incorrectly; rather you need to demonstrate that everything was done correctly as per the terms of the project contract.

## 4.10 Conclusion

The success and credibility of your EU-funded project relies on your management of it. By planning and managing budgets regularly reporting on performance, addressing risks and ensuring long-term financial sustainability you can ensure that you and your consortium's endeavours remain feasible cost-effective and impactful.

**C.-Andreas Dalluege** Founder and Managing Partner of IBK Group; Chairman of the European Business Excellence Network e.V.; National Council Member of the Irish Work Study Institute. Certified Advisor & Trainer of EFQM, Operating Partner and Trainer of Initiative Ludwig-Erhard-Preis (ILEP).

Since 1990 he participated as the senior researcher for his organisation in over 35 EU projects in most programme types offered by the EU and represented his company in all of them at the Management Board level as well as worked as our lead researcher in them.

He serves on the national board of the Irish Work Study Institute (IIESMS) and as President of the European Business Excellence Network (EuroBEN).

As a lecturer at the TH Aschaffenburg, he also gives classes on the design, proposing and running of EU Research projects since 2019. Contact: cad@ibk.eu

**Aleksandra Lovrenčič** MSc is the Head of the International Cooperation and Research Affairs Office as well as the Erasmus Co-ordinator at the University of Maribor, Faculty of Health Sciences in Slovenia. Aleksandra oversees Erasmus+ mobility for students and employees, activities of international cooperation of the faculty, and offers support to the Vice Dean in overviewing the faculty's research work. She also organises international and domestic conferences, congresses, summer schools and other events. She operates the faculty's social media, works on different publications and manages various national and international projects. She is a member of the European Association of Research Managers and Administrators (EARMA). Contact: aleksandra.lovrencic@um.si

**Florian Scheibein** is a Research Assistant and PhD student at the School of Health Sciences, South East Technological University. He is currently the Lead Research Assistant for an EU4Health project—DDS-MAP—and Grant Holder Manager for an EU COST Action—CUPID. He has been involved in three ERASMUS projects and was the co-recipient of the Council of Europe Pompidou Group European Drug Prevention Prize for one of these projects. He is an Editor for the Harm Reduction Journal and is a Co-Director and General Secretary of the Network of Early Career Professionals in Addiction Medicine which works with the World Health Organisation's Alcohol, Drugs and Addictive Behaviours Unit. Contact: Florian.Scheibein@setu.ie

# Chapter 5
# Starting the Project

**C.-Andreas Dalluege and John Stephen Gary Wells**

Starting your project is an exciting and critical phase in the life cycle of any EU-funded project. In this section, we explore key aspects for starting your project, including the project 'Kick Off' meeting, establishing project management structures, project manual, developing work plans, and engaging stakeholders.

## 5.1 Starting the Project: The 'Kick Off' Meeting

Your 'Kick Off' Meeting initiates the start of the project. It fosters collaboration between project partners, stakeholders, and the funding agency. In this meeting, all project partners and relevant representatives from the funding agency will come together to discuss how the project will proceed, align expectations, establish communication channels, and set the foundation for a harmonious collaboration.

We have experienced both online 'kick off' meetings and in-person 'kick off' meetings. Based on our experience the most effective 'kick off' meetings are in person at a specified venue since they facilitate interpersonal relationship building between partners over coffee breaks, lunch, and after the meeting has finished. Online meetings tend to be formal and formulaic with little opportunity for partners to get to know one another beyond the project agenda. They are also highly susceptible to technical challenges (such as slow internet connections) and we often find

C.-A. Dalluege
IBK, Wiesbaden, Germany
e-mail: cad@ibk.eu

J. S. G. Wells (✉)
South East Technological University, Waterford, Ireland
e-mail: john.wells@setu.ie



C.-A. Dalluege, J. S. G. Wells (eds.), *Navigating an EU Research Project*, Management for Professionals, https://doi.org/10.1007/978-3-031-70928-9_5

that those in attendance online are often distracted by other factors related to their workspace (for example, reading and answering their day-to-day work emails!)

### 5.1.1 Preparing the 'Kick Off' Meeting

The first step in organising a 'Kick Off' meeting is to develop a clear and comprehensive agenda that outlines the objectives, topics, and activities for the meeting. The agenda should cover the following key aspects:

- **Project Overview**: Provide a brief overview of the project, its goals, objectives, and expected outcomes. This will help to ensure that all participants have a shared understanding of the project's purpose and direction.
- Co**nsortium introductions**: Allocate time for each partner organisation to introduce themselves and their role within the project consortium. This helps to establish personal connections and foster a sense of team spirit among the partners.
- **Work packages and tasks**: Review the project's work packages, tasks, and deliverables. Also, discuss and clarify the roles and responsibilities of each partner organisation and discuss any potential challenges or risks.
- **Project management and coordination**: Discuss the project's management and coordination structure, including the roles and responsibilities of the project co-ordinator, work-package leaders, and other key personnel and who within the consortium will take on these overall management roles.
- For example, we establish three management boards—the Project Management Board, the Technical Management Board, and the Advisory Board (we provide more detail on these below). The Project Co-ordinator normally chairs the Project Management Board. Membership and roles of these Boards should be approved formally at the 'Kick off' meeting.
- **Project manual:** We advise that you develop a draft project manual that you then present for comment, amendment, and approval. The manual provides a written set of guidelines for the management of the project. We provide more detail on this later in this chapter.
- **Communication and dissemination**: Outline the project's communication and dissemination strategy, including internal communication channels, establishment of a project website (which is usually required by EU funders), external outreach activities, and any relevant branding or marketing materials.
- **Financial and administrative matters**: Address the project's financial and administrative requirements, including budget allocations, financial reporting, and any relevant regulations or guidelines.
- **Timeline and milestones**: Review the project's timeline, milestones, and key deadlines, ensuring that all partners have a clear understanding of the project's schedule and their individual responsibilities.

Remember that the 'Kick Off' meeting is just the beginning of the project journey. To maintain momentum and ensure that the project stays on track, it is important to follow up on the outcomes of the meeting. Consider the following steps for effective follow-up:

- **Meeting minutes and action points**: Document the meeting through minutes. We recommend for the kick off meeting you ask a colleague from your institution to take the minutes. Use a standardised template that can be used to minute subsequent meetings over the course of your project. Having a standardised template will greatly help you when writing up the narrative of the project for the interim and final reports to the funder.

- The minutes should be outcomes focused rather than a detailed 'he said/she said' narrative. Record key decisions, action points, and assigned responsibilities, providing a clear record of the meeting's outcomes and especially indicating a 'to-do list' with responsibilities and deadlines for the next activities.

- Aim to distribute the minutes within 3 working days of the meeting to all project partners (this should be your target for subsequent meetings). By distributing the minute within 3 working days, you convey a message to partners about your personal efficiency and convey to partners an overall message about efficient project performance.
- **Establishing communication channels**: Set up an agreed-upon communication channel for the project consortium. This can be an email list, use of an online platform (for example, most projects are expected to set up a project website and this could be used), or project management tools of which there are many and each has its strengths and weaknesses.
- For example, within the SSTeMM project we principally used email and Dropbox. For DDS-MAP, which has extensive number of partners—15 in total, we use Zoom for monthly and working group meetings and Trello to work on and store documents.
- Inform all partners about these channels, are able to access, and use them effectively. Some partners may have varying views or negative experiences with some tools, so it is important to reach a collective consensus, which tools to use so discuss these at the 'Kick Off' meeting. If you do not achieve consensus, you will find that relationships and project efficiency quickly break down.
- **Monitoring progress:** At the 'Kick Off' meeting agree upon a standardised one-page project progress-monitoring template. Each work-package leader then completes and returns this to the Technical Board (see below) on a monthly basis until the work package is complete. This document helps to ensure that partners remain accountable and that the project stays on track. It ensures that any delay or problem is quickly identified and can be addressed.

In conclusion, the 'Kick Off' meeting is a crucial event to start an EU-funded project, establishing the foundations for a successful partnership and setting the tone for the project's collaboration. By carefully planning and organising the meeting, engaging participants, and following up on the outcomes, project co-ordinators can lay the groundwork for a productive and impactful project journey. Investing time and effort in the 'Kick Off' meeting ultimately contributes to the overall success of the project, helping to achieve the broader goals of the EU-funding programme and create lasting positive impacts for the target audience and stakeholders.

## 5.2 The Project Manual

As we said when describing the 'Kick Off' meeting, a draft of the Project Manual should be prepared prior to the meeting and then discussed, amended, and approved formally. The project manual is an essential tool for ensuring the successful implementation and management of any project. It serves as a comprehensive guide, outlining the project's objectives, tasks, procedures, and responsibilities and providing partners with a clear roadmap for their collaboration. This section will explore the key components of a project manual and offer guidance on how to create an effective and user-friendly resource for your project consortium.

We structure our project manuals as follows:

1. Introduction (Objectives and Scope)
2. Partner Details
3. Project Management
4. Project Meetings
5. Conflict Resolution Procedures
6. Structure and Deadlines of Administrative Documents and Financing
7. Project Dissemination and Communication Plan
8. Work-Package Reporting
9. Quality Management
10. Project GANTT
11. Project Budget

Below we describe in more detail what each of these 11 sections shown in Fig. 5.1 includes within the project manual:

(1) **Introduction (Objectives and Scope)**: Begin by stating that the provenance and formal status of the manual, that is it is there to provide the definitive guideline which will be the reference document for project that it has been agreed by the consortium and was formally approved at the 'Kick Off' meeting. Describe how the project manual will support and maintain the project's operation.

You then outline the project's overall objectives and scope. Provide a clear and concise overview of the project's purpose, goals, and expected outcomes.

(2) **Partner details:** List the contact details of each partner including the name of the organisation and its website, the appointed partner project lead, and the team working with them (include a phone number for the project lead partner and email contacts for everyone involved). Then list the membership of the Project Management Board, the Technical Board, and the Advisory Board

**Table of Content**

| | |
|---|---|
| **1 Introduction** | **6 Structure and Deadlines of Administrative Documents** |
| **2 Partner Details** | 6.1 Document Types and their Deadlines |
| 2.1 Co-ordinator of the Project | 6.2 Format of Partners' Contributions |
| 2.2 Project Partners | 6.3 Monthly Status Report (MSR) |
| 2.3 EC Project Officer | 6.3.1 Review Cycle |
| 2.4 Associated, non-funded Partners | 6.3.2 Structure |
| **3 Project Management** | 6.4 Quarterly Progress Report (QPR) |
| 3.1 Management Structure | 6.4.1 Review Cycle |
| 3.2 Conflict Resolution Procedures | 6.4.2 Structure |
| 3.3 Management Tools | 6.5 Interim and Final Report |
| 3.3.1 Project Management | 6.6 Cost Statements |
| 3.3.2 Office & Productivity Tools | **7 Work Package Report** |
| 3.3.3 Communication Tools and Procedures | 7.1 Responsibility & Co-ordination |
| **4 Fore- & Background Materials** | 7.2 Review Cycle |
| | 7.2 Proposed Structure |
| **5 Document Format and Numbering** | 7.3 Submission Procedure |

**Fig. 5.1** Contents page of a project manual

members. In the case of the latter, provide the names of their respective organisations and contact emails.

(3) **Project management**: Describe the project's organisational structure, including the roles and responsibilities of the project co-ordinator, work-package leaders, and other key personnel. This should include an organisational chart, illustrating the hierarchical relationships between the various partners and roles. Describe guidelines/principles for internal communication and between the partners of the project consortium. This may include details on the following:

- Communication Channels: Specify the channels and tools that partners should use for internal communication, such as email, online platforms, or project management software.
- Meeting Schedules: Outline the schedule for regular consortium meetings, workshops, and virtual check-ins, specifying the frequency, format, and expected attendees.

(4) **Project meetings**: Outline the nature of the type of formal project meetings scheduled over the lifetime of the project as these relate to project management. State how frequently they should be, the rules of attendance, and who can vote for each partner organisation at what level of meeting type.

Describe meetings which are face-to-face and which ones are virtual or hybrid to minimise environmental impact and travel cost. Normally there should be three face-to-face meetings (the costs of which should be included in your approved budget). These are the 'Kick Off' meeting, an interim project meeting, and an end of project meeting/final 'conference' meeting.

(5) **Risk resolution procedures**: The PMB is responsible for managing overall risk management. Describe the potential/foreseen risks and challenges that the

project may encounter. Outline procedures for identifying, assessing, and mitigating these risks. These may include:

- Risk Identification: Provide guidance on the process for identifying potential risks, including the use of risk registers or other tools.
- Risk Assessment: Outline the criteria for assessing the likelihood and impact of identified risks, and state the process for reporting these risks once identified and how risks will be prioritised.
- Risk Mitigation: Describe the strategies and measures that partners should take to mitigate and manage identified risks, including contingency plans and potential corrective actions.
- Risk Resolution: Action of each risk level based on impact or costs.
- Conflict Resolution: Describe both informal and formal processes for conflict resolution should this arise between partners. Formal conflict resolution procedures are located PMB. Informal resolution is located at the PTB level.

(6) **Structure and deadlines of administrative documents and financing**: Describe the procedures and templates for reporting project progress, deliverables, and financial matters. Include the frequency and deadlines for submitting reports both internal and external to the EU Funders.

Describe project's documentation and recordkeeping requirement that will ensure that partners maintain accurate and up-to-date records of their activities and outputs. This may involve:

- Templates and Formats: Specify the templates and formats that partners should use for documenting their work, such as progress reports, deliverable templates, or meeting minutes.
- Recordkeeping Systems: Describe the systems and tools that partners should use for storing and managing project documentation, such as shared drives, online platforms, etc.
- Financial Reporting: Outline the procedures and templates for financial reporting, including the frequency and deadlines for submitting financial reports.
- Monitoring and Evaluation: Include a section on monitoring and evaluation, describing the processes and tools for assessing the project's progress, achievements, and impact. Outline the tools and processes that partners should use to monitor the project's progress, such as progress reports, performance dashboards, or regular check-ins with the project management boards.

(7) **Project dissemination and communication plan**: Provide an overview of the project's dissemination and exploitation strategy. Dissemination and external communication (such as a constantly updated project website—see the SSTeMM website as an example at www.sstemm.eu) is usually a required deliverable and part of a work-package schedule of work.

As part of the narrative explain how the project's results and outputs will be shared with relevant stakeholders and used to create lasting impact. This may include:

- Target Audiences: Identify the target audiences for the project's dissemination and exploitation activities, such as policymakers, practitioners, or end-users.
- Dissemination Channels: Specify the channels and platforms that will be used to share the project's results and outputs, such as conferences, publications, websites, or social media.
- Exploitation Plans: Describe the plans for using the project's results and outputs to create tangible impact, such as developing new products or services, influencing policy, or improving practices in the target sector.

(8) **Work-package reporting**: Describe each work package and what each work package's aim and deliverables encompass. Specify the roles and responsibilities of each partner organisation in relation to each work package. Include each one's timeline, outlining the expected completion dates for each task within the work package and any dependencies or interconnections between tasks across work packages.

(9) **Quality Management**: Establish a quality assurance framework for the project, outlining the processes, procedures, and criteria for ensuring the quality and integrity of the project's outputs and outcomes. This may include:

- Quality Standards: Describe the quality standards and benchmarks that the project's deliverables and activities should adhere to, such as industry standards, best practices, or regulatory requirements.
- Quality Control: Describe the procedures for reviewing and evaluating the project's outputs and activities, including the roles and responsibilities of the partners in this process.
- Data Protection and Security: Address any data protection and security requirements that partners should be aware of, including compliance with relevant legislation, such as the General Data Protection Regulation (GDPR).
- Quality Gates (QG): Within our projects, we use the concept of Quality Gates as a control mechanism to close formally each operational work package. The QG is based on a survey of all partners where they vote on the degree of completion of each task within a Work Package.

The QG passes if the overall accumulated vote reaches an agreement of over 90%. If the survey result falls below the 90% threshold, a workshop is conducted to resolve the open issues behind the failure to meet the threshold.

In tasks where external test users or pilots are involved, they will additionally become involved in the results evaluation through feed-back reports and a formal survey.

(10) **Project GANTT**: The project GANTT exists in a condensed version for fast overview, just listing WPs and project quarters (see Fig. 5.2 above)

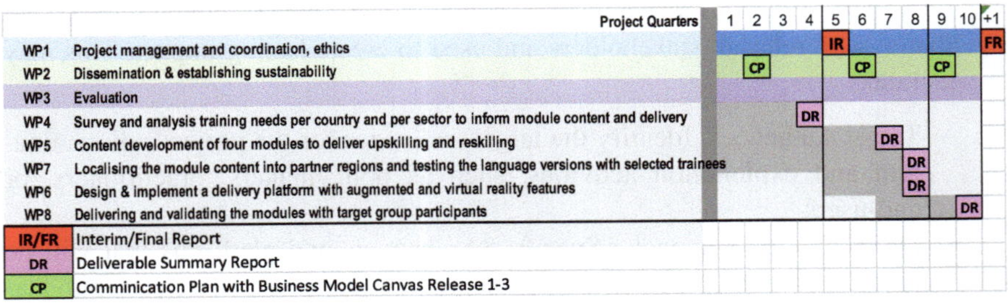


**Fig. 5.2** Compact project GANTT

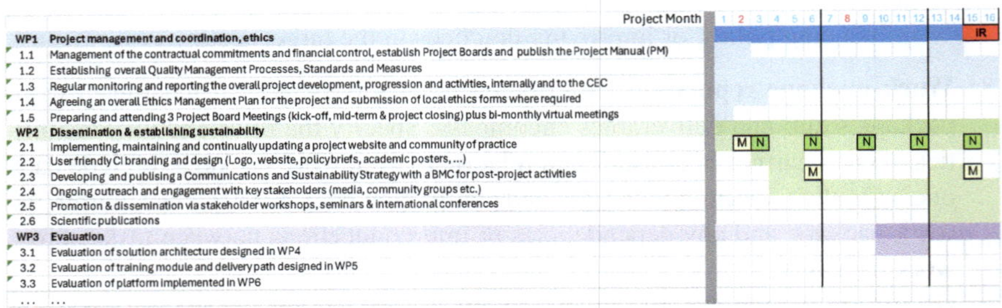


**Fig. 5.3** Detailed project GANTT

Additionally, a detailed version goes down to the task level and show activities on a month-by-month level (see Fig. 5.3 below).

(11) **Project budget**: Provide a budget overview, detailing the distribution over all work packages by partner. You can take this directly from your proposal document. If any budget changes requested by the EU Project Office, both the original requested budget and final one after such a change is given. This is to ensure that minor budget changes between partner allocations required by the EU project office post your award of funds are not disputed later in the project trajectory.

If the budget information is also provided in the format of the original planning spreadsheet, then each partner can transfer it easily into a resource tracking tool for their own organisation as shown in the example below (Fig. 5.4).

In conclusion, by carefully tailoring the project manual to the specific needs and context of your EU-funded project, you can create a valuable resource that supports effective project management and collaboration. Ultimately, a well-structured and comprehensive project manual can contribute to the overall success of your project, helping to achieve the broader goals of the EU-funding programme and create lasting positive impacts for your target audience and stakeholders.

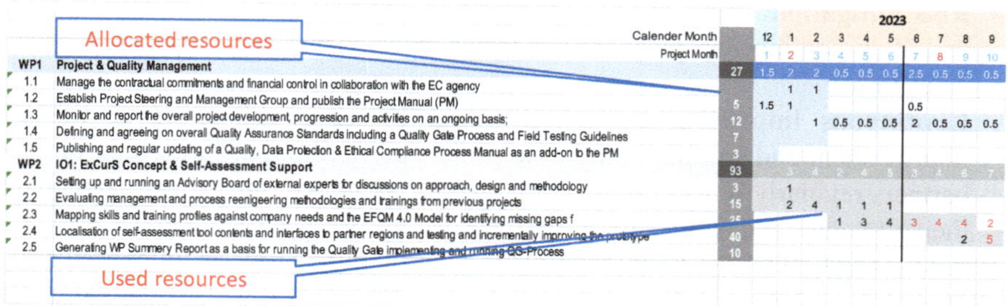


**Fig. 5.4** Resource planning and tracking

## 5.3 Operationalising the Project Structure

The 'Kick Off' Meeting initiates the implementation of your project, starting with Resource Management. This consists of the following:

- **Financial management:** Financial management will involve budget tracking, expense approval, and financial reporting. Ensure that all project partners are aware of and comply with these processes and any financial regulations associated with the funding agency.
- **Human resources**: Each partner organisation is responsible for their own human resource management. However, as the coordinating partner you must keep an overview of human resources within the project to ensure these are corresponding to the project tasks with which each partner is concerned.
- **Equipment and infrastructure:** Within the given budget, each partner is autonomous in their project-specific investments. So you as co-ordinator are not the decision maker in this area. Therefore, it is important that you work closely with your consortium partners to ensure that equipment that they purchase are appropriate for the tasks carried out.

Implementing your risk management plan is an important operational management tool for the successful completion of your project. This is because a well-crafted risk management plan will identify, assess, and mitigate potential risks and challenges throughout the project's lifecycle. I

Your risk management plan should identify potential risks associated with the project's implementation, including financial, operational, technical, legal, and reputational risks. Operationally, the plan should do the following:

- **Monitoring and evaluation**: Use the monitoring and evaluation framework to track progress, assess the project's impact, and identify areas for improvement. Regularly review and update this framework to ensure that it remains relevant and effective.
- **Risk assessment:** Assess the likelihood and potential impact of each identified risk, prioritising risks according to their severity and the potential harm they may cause to the project.

- **Risk mitigation:** Develop and implement strategies to mitigate identified risks, including contingency plans, risk transfer mechanisms, and other appropriate measures.
- **Continuous improvement and learning**: Foster a culture of continuous improvement and learning within the project consortium, ensuring that project partners regularly reflect on their experiences, share lessons learned, and adapt their strategies and approaches as needed.
- **Knowledge sharing:** Encourage project partners to share their experiences, insights, and best practices with each other and with the wider community of EU-funded projects. Attend workshops, webinars, conferences, and other knowledge-sharing platforms to gather intelligence on risks experienced and managed by others. Such activities will provide you with insights as to how other projects are managing similar risks to ones your project may experience and thereby better inform your own risk mitigation approaches.
- **Adaptation and iteration**: Be prepared to adapt and iterate the project's strategies and approaches based on the feedback, lessons learned, and emerging trends and challenges as the project progresses. This will help to ensure that the project remains relevant, effective, and aligned with the needs and interests of its target audience and stakeholders.

## 5.4 Establishing the Project Management Boards and Their Role

To implement the above, you will need to implement the management oversight structures that you will have outlined in your proposal. You will formally have agreed these structures with your partners at the 'Kick Off' meeting.

Typically, two management boards that will manage the project are the Project Management Board (PMB, chaired by the Project Co-ordinator) and the Technical Management Board (PTB) of the project. An Advisory Board, chaired by and consisting of members who are independent of the project, will support these management boards (see Fig. 5.5).

The Project Management Board, chaired by the Project Co-ordinator (PC), and consisting of the respective project leads from each consortium partner, the PMB will be the main decision-making body and you should set up a schedule of meetings of the PMB across the lifetime of your project.

The PMB primary task is the effective and timely coordination of all project activities and successful financial, administrative, and technical management ensuring the following:

- The overall objectives of the project are accomplished within the timeframe agreed;
- All project activities are carefully monitored to ensure project progress;
- An effective internal communication strategy is designed;

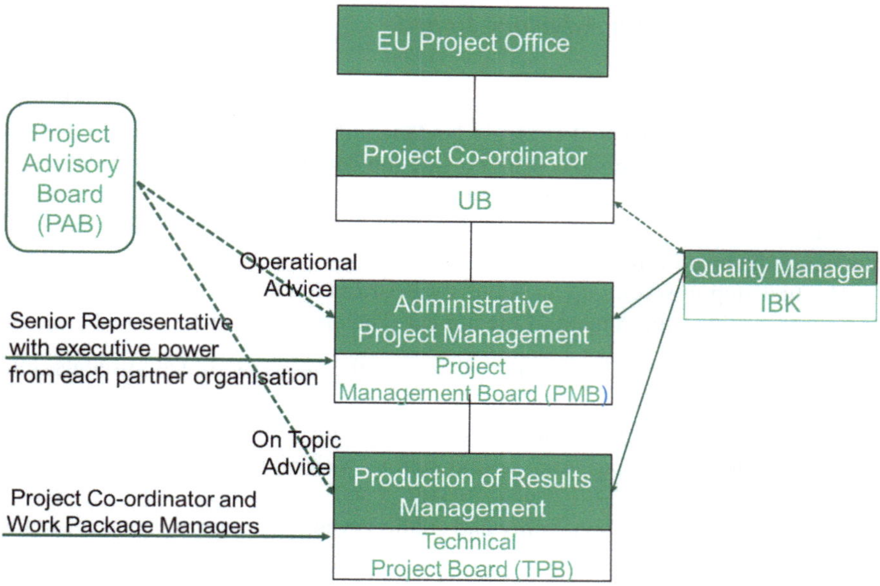


**Fig. 5.5** Project management & governance structure used in our projects

- Project partners get the necessary support to complete their tasks throughout the project lifecycle;
- A partner agreement is signed by all partners;
- The required financial and administrative reports are prepared;
- All contractual and reporting matters between the Project and the EU project office run properly and smoothly.

The Technical Management Board (TMB) manages the operational side of the project. It oversees and coordinates the efforts of the working groups. The membership of this board consists of the work-package leaders who agree a chairperson drawn from their number. The TMB is answerable to the PMB. The TMB should set up a schedule of meetings reflective of the work-package timelines in order to ensure effective oversight of these. The TMB carries out the following:

- That all partners deliver the required outcomes within the set timeframe.
- That effective monitoring of the scheduled activities mitigates unnecessary delays to project outputs.
- That on-going risk assessment identifies potential problem areas and defines appropriate corrective actions if required.
- That evaluation of project outcomes ensures appropriateness and relevance in all partner countries.
- That rigorous quality management ensures that project aims and objectives as stated in the approved funded proposal are met.

### *5.4.1 Setting Up an Advisory Board*

An Advisory Board is a group of experts, stakeholders, and other relevant individuals who provide independent strategic guidance, input, and support to the project consortium. They are recruited from outside the consortium partnership. This section will discuss the key aspects of setting up an Advisory Board, including determining its objectives, selecting members, defining roles and responsibilities, and managing the board effectively.

The first step in setting up an Advisory Board is to clearly define its objectives and purpose within the context of the project. The objectives may include:

- Providing strategic guidance and advice on the project's direction, goals, and activities.
- Identifying potential risks and opportunities for the project.
- Facilitating networking and collaboration with external stakeholders and organisations.
- Enhancing the project's visibility and credibility among target audiences and the broader community.
- Ensuring the project's alignment with current sectoral trends, best practices, and stakeholder needs.
- The composition of the Advisory Board is crucial to its effectiveness. When selecting members, consider the following factors:
- **Expertise:** Choose individuals with relevant knowledge and experience in the project's subject matter, industry, or target audience. This can include experts from academia, industry, government, and civil society.
- **Diversity:** Aim for a diverse board that includes members from different sectors, backgrounds, and perspectives. This can help to ensure that the board provides well-rounded and balanced advice.
- **Regional Distribution:** Addressing a region that is not covered by the geographic spread of the consortium partners.
- **Commitment:** Select members who are genuinely interested in the project's success and are willing to devote time and effort to support the project.
- **Networking Potential**: Consider members who have strong connections to key stakeholders, organisations, or communities that may be beneficial to the project.

Clearly define the role and responsibilities of the Advisory Board Members to ensure that they understand their function and expectations. Such roles and responsibilities may include:

- Providing strategic guidance and recommendations on the project's direction, goals, and activities.
- Identifying potential risks, opportunities, and emerging trends that may affect the project.
- Supporting the project's communication and dissemination efforts by promoting the project within their networks and communities.
- Participating in regular board meetings and other relevant project events.

Effective management of the Advisory Board is essential to ensure its on-going value and impact on the project. Consider the following strategies for managing the board:

- **Appoint a chairperson**: Appoint a chairperson to lead the Board. Board Members can elect a chairperson from their number, though we usually approach a recognised leader in the field that we are investigating and ask them to act as Chairperson prior to setting up the board. In our experience, it is rare that such a person refuses.
- **Board Meetings**: Organise regular board meetings (e.g., quarterly, biannually) to discuss the project's progress, challenges, and opportunities with members of the PMB. These meetings can be held in person or virtually, depending on the board members' availability and preferences.
- **Clear Communication**: Establish clear communication channels and protocols for sharing information and updates with advisory board members. This can include regular newsletters, email updates, and dedicated online platforms.
- **Engaging Board Members**: Actively engage board members in discussing the project's activities and decision-making, to ensure that their expertise and perspectives are valued.
- **Evaluation and Feedback**: Regularly evaluate the effectiveness of the Advisory Board and solicit feedback from board members on their experiences and suggestions for improvement.

Maximise the value and impact of the Advisory Board by leveraging its expertise and networks to support the project's implementation and dissemination efforts. This can include:

- **Collaboration and networking**: Encourage knowledge exchange between the advisory board and the consortium. This will serve to build new network connectivity post project completion. For example, advisory board members can introduce you to new partners or indicate where new opportunities for your project exist.
- **Promotion**: Leverage the credibility and influence of the board members to enhance the project's visibility and reputation among target audiences and the broader community. This can involve having board members speak at conferences, write articles or op-eds, or share project updates through their professional networks and social media channels.
- **Capacity Building**: Draw on the board members' expertise to provide capacity building and training opportunities for the project consortium and other stakeholders. This can include workshops, webinars, and mentoring sessions on various topics relevant to the project's goals and activities.

It is important for building and maintaining your networks to acknowledge the contributions of the Advisory Board members. You can do this by recognising their efforts and commitment to the project's success, both within your reports to the EU Project Office and in the project's public communications.

Setting up an Advisory Board can significantly contribute to the success of an EU-funded project by providing strategic guidance, expertise, and support. By carefully considering the objectives, selecting members, defining roles and responsibilities, and effectively managing the board, project consortia can maximise the value and impact of their Advisory Boards. This investment in strategic guidance and collaboration can ultimately enhance the project's outcomes, helping to achieve the broader goals of the EU-funding programme and impact positively on your target audience and stakeholders.

To summarise, establishing your project management structures and responsibilities of individuals from within the consortium is a key element in the overall operational success of your project (see Fig. 5.6 which sets out relationships). Establishing clear lines of communication and accountability within these relationships will greatly enhance implementation of your work packages, manage risks, and ensure deliverables hit deadlines.

## 5.5 Managing Expectations

European Union projects involve partners from different countries, cultures, and professional backgrounds. This diversity brings both opportunities and challenges in managing expectations among project partners. In this section, we explore these opportunities and challenges and offer guidance in navigating these complexities.

Partners from different countries may have distinct cultural norms, communication styles, and work habits. These factors can influence their expectations regarding project management, decision-making processes, and collaboration. For

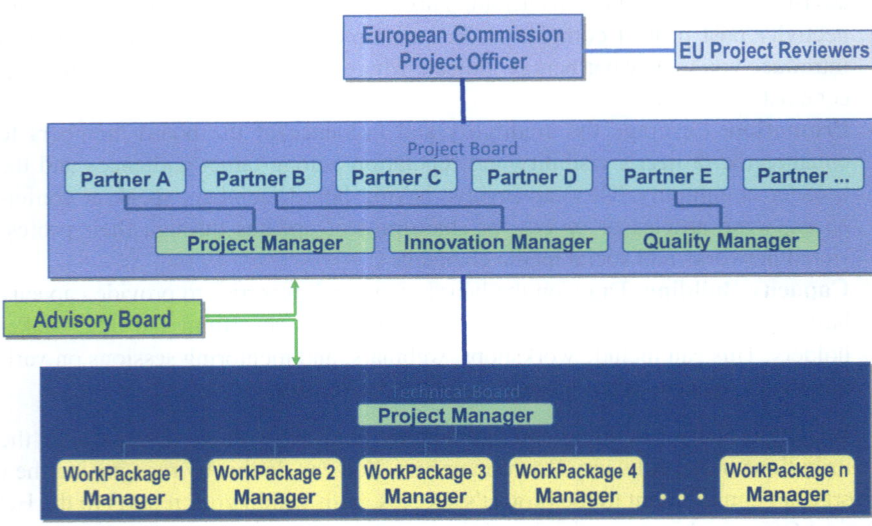


**Fig. 5.6** Operative project structure

instance, we recall an incident from a project where one of our partners faced an issue with the UK project lead. To address this concern, they expressed their grievances during a meeting, with the Project Board. After listing all their concerns, they stood up without saying another word and left the room—a behaviour that surprised our partners from south European countries who felt it lacked tact.

Just before the atmosphere could completely sour another partner explained that the partner who had left the room had acted tactfully and respectfully according to their culture. The other partner explained to the consortium that in seeking a 'solution', between the two parties the partner who had left expressed his feelings in a forum dedicated to such matters. Since the issue he wanted resolved concerned the consortium he listed all his points to ensure no problems were left unaddressed. He then stepped out of the room to give the group an opportunity to express their grievances without having to be polite towards him.

He expected to be called back for a positive discussion free from emotional distractions. Once this understanding was established the 'problem' could be easily resolved. Without this explanation it would have been challenging to find a solution.

Partners from organisations such as Non-Government Organisations or private companies may have priorities, resources, and approaches when implementing projects. These differences can shape their expectations regarding project outcomes and processes in terms of outreach and post project utilisation of results. Ownership rights over parts of the project outcomes and potential financial gain under such conditions can also be significant considerations where publication of what they might deem information that threatens their commercial interests may become an issue between them and academic partners (whose career progression and expectations of their universities is to publish).

It is important to familiarise yourself with your business/private organisations' and university partners' expectations in these matters and have an open discussion in relation to what the EU will allow in this regard and what the consortium can decide independently of the EU on these matters. This will help to avoid later arguments. This should be part of the 'Kick Off' meeting conversation and guidelines on this matter included in your dissemination rules within the Project Manual. We would also advise stating a guide on order of authorship for publications arising from the project.

Establishing open and honest communication is crucial for managing expectations in projects funded by the European Union. It is important to encourage partners to share their perspectives, concerns, and aspirations while fostering an environment of respect and understanding. To promote this kind of communication consider implementing these strategies:

- **Check-ins**: Organise meetings, workshops, or virtual check-ins where partners can update each other on their progress, discuss challenges they are facing and exchange ideas.
- **Create space for feedback**: Encourage all partners to provide feedback on the project's progress and processes. Make sure that everyone feels comfortable sharing their perspectives without fear of judgement or reprisal.

- **Encouraging listening**: Foster a culture, within the project consortium where all partners engage in active listening. This means seeking to understand each other's perspectives than simply waiting for an opportunity to speak.

To ensure that everyone is working towards a shared goal it is essential to establish a shared vision and objectives for the project. While the initial proposal already provides some guidance, it's important to acknowledge that a lot can change during the year between proposal and project commencement in our fast-paced world. Therefore, it is necessary to review and refine the project's goals and objectives as a process involving all partners.

This starts at the 'Kick Off' meeting but you should also see it as an on-going process, where you as project co-ordinator have a special responsibility to ensure it is an on-going process over the project's life time.

You should encourage partners to talk about their understanding of the project's primary aims and the broader context within which it operates. This will help to develop an achievable shared focus on concrete and measurable outcomes. It is important to note that while we strive to address partner expectations and priorities as much as possible there may be limitations due to contractual obligations, with the EU.

To create shared achievable goals revisit and refine goals based on partner feedback and input. It is crucial to ensure that any changes align with the defined objectives from the proposal to safeguard your funding. To encourage a shared across partner view do the following:

- Recognise that partners may have expectations so proactively identify potential areas of divergence or disagreement, within project goals to establish common ground.
- Develop a project plan that allows for adaptability acknowledging that partner expectations and priorities may evolve throughout the course of the project.
- Ensure all partners have an opportunity to contribute their insights and expertise to the project valuing their perspectives and integrate them into activities and outcomes, if possible.
- Acknowledge that expectations may change over time and commit to actively monitoring them throughout the project's duration and making adjustments as necessary.

Here are some strategies to consider when monitoring and managing expectations:

- Conduct progress reviews to assess the project's accomplishments, challenges, and alignment with the expectations of partners. This might involve adjustments to objectives, methodologies, or expected outcomes as necessary.
- Encourage partners to engage in dialogue and reflection about their expectations and experiences throughout the project. This fosters a culture of learning and adaptation.
- Proactively address any emerging issues or discrepancies between partner expectations by working to find solutions. Maintaining a constructive project environment is crucial.

To conclude, managing expectations is essential for your success. By promoting communication and dialogue to establish a shared vision and goals you will create an inclusive project that recognises and conciliates difference. By adjusting to expectations a shared view, you can navigate complexities successfully.

## 5.6 Project Operations Through KPIs and Risk Management

Project operations convert objectives into actions. In this section, we explore and offer advice on how to create and implement operational plans that yield positive results in relation to roles, responsibilities, and risk management.

As we have emphasised regularly, define the roles and responsibilities of each project partner based on their expertise, resources, and capabilities. When defining these roles and responsibilities do the following:

- Clearly identify who will oversee the management and coordination of the project and any subcomponents or work packages.
- Assign specific tasks and deliverables to individual partners based on their expertise and capacity.

Review the work plan described in the proposal and adjust it to accommodate changes in the environment since it was submitted (remember changes can occur to this plan by requests from the EU as a condition of funding or certain things can have changed between submission and commencement of the project—the timeline between these is usually a year).

Part of this review includes considering resource allocations, personnel, and materials. When allocating resources for your project keep the following factors in mind:

- Minor adjustments to the budget may need to be agreed based on the work re-alignment to reflect changes within partner organisations since the submission or to accommodate EU requests for change. The EU project office needs to agree to all changes, so make sure you inform them of your intent.
- During the proposal phase, for the purposes of budgeting, a virtual headcount may be used for cost calculations. This is now operationalised to individuals from partner organisations who possess skills, expertise, and availability along with any additional personnel that may be required. Such an operationalisation may affect person day costings.
- Identify any material resources such as equipment, software tools, or facilities that are vital, for successful implementation of the project. During the proposal phase the cost for each type of investment is based on thorough market research. However, bearing in mind the passage of time between submission and implementation these costs may have risen. You do have some flexibility to adjust the expenditure by incorporating market prices for the required equipment.

Monitoring and evaluation processes play a crucial role in tracking the progress of the project. Here are some key considerations when implementing monitoring and evaluation procedures:

- Define a set of Key Performance Indicators (KPIs) that will be used to measure progress and success. These may include achieving milestones delivering high quality outcomes or reaching a number of beneficiaries.
- Incorporate the KPIS into the tools and techniques for monitoring progress, such as monthly or quarterly reports, time sheets, performance dashboards, or regular 'check-ins' with project partners.
- Outline the criteria, methods, and data sources for assessment. This evaluation framework should align with the project's objectives. Provide insights into its effectiveness, efficiency, and sustainability.
- Incorporate the KPIs into the QGs to assess the achievement of each Work Package or Intellectual.

### 5.6.1 *Risk Management*

Since projects have a life span of between two to four years, unexpected events can arise. In the case of the SSTeMM project, we experienced the impact of a pandemic, which made it impossible for partners to travel and disrupted planned meetings, with pilot users and in-person multiplier events (a multiplier event is a dissemination meeting focused on spreading information about the project to sectors that might have interest in your project). This situation also had an effect on the field-testing phase, which was originally supposed to cover a third of the project's time and resources and serve as a basis for validating results of SSTeMM.

We would emphasise two things in relation to thinking about risks—how to manage foreseeable risks and what you will do, should an unforeseen risk arise. Risks that are possible to foresee include changes in personnel within the project over time; delays if you must engage with outside parties, for example agreeing on access to a group through a third party or seeking ethics approval. In relation to the latter, incorporate these considerations into your timeline planning.

If the timeline is not met, consider with partners how timelines elsewhere can be shortened or whether adjust operations to get around the delay. With regard to changes in personnel, if there is a considerable delay in replacement consider reallocating work to other partners with cognate skills set.

In relation to unforeseen risks consult with partners as to the level of threat this poses to project operations and timelines. If small risks, then manage them 'within house'. However, if significant, then consult with your EU Project office about it. You will find that they are generally helpful. Thus, when the Covid lockdown happened in the SSTeMM project we immediately engaged with the Project Office (in our case this was the Irish National Agency) about our challenges. We found them helpful in their responses and through regular dialogue; they supported all the changes we made in terms of operations and timelines to take account of the new operating environment in which we found ourselves.

To address conflicts that may arise in teams due to differing opinions or cultural disparities it is important to handle them in a respectful manner. When working in groups effective communication entails being sensitive to the language skills, communication preferences, and behavioural norms of team members.

As a mechanism for managing these differences, you should acknowledge they exist within your risk management and conflict resolution plan. Describe expected norms of behaviour agreed between partners in terms of conduct within the project. Also, specify a process for the management of disputes between individuals within your consortium.

To summarise, by implementing a forward-thinking strategy, towards planning, project co-ordinators, and collaborators can amplify the effectiveness, efficiency, and influence of their projects. This approach guarantees the fulfilment of commitments and aids in achieving the European Union's priorities and objectives.

## 5.7 Creating the Research Team Milieu: Nurturing a Collaborative and Productive Environment

Creating an environment that nurtures collaboration and productivity is essential when building your consortium and interacting with partners, from different countries and disciplines. In this section, we explore strategies and principles that can help foster a collaborative and inclusive research team environment.

As we have previously stated building a shared vision between partners goes a long way to establishing good relations between individuals and partners. For example, we have been involved with project co-ordinators who have failed to explain their vision for the project or lacked clarity about the sustainability of outcomes. The result has been poor relations and understanding between partners leading to a tense operational environment. For example, we observed one project in which some of us were involved where the operational environment was so tense that one partner pulled out of the project. Such an action is extreme and not easily explained to the funder in your final report as a mark of success!

It is crucial therefore not only to involve project partners from the beginning to co-create shared vision but also to have clarity in your own mind about the vision in terms of how and what you want to achieve and communicate this. If you are unsure, this quickly will become apparent to your partners and sow seeds of doubt in their minds that you, as co-ordinator, are not fully in command of the project agenda and its direction. Lack of confidence in your vision by partners can in turn lead to lack of confidence in your overall project leadership role. Thereby facilitating regular disagreements between partners.

Open effective communication plays a role in maintaining a positive team environment and confidence in your leadership as co-ordinator and good relationships between partners. Openly sharing information, data, and insights is crucial. Create an environment that encourages team members to express their ideas, concerns, and suggestions while fostering respect and trust. In teams with norms and communication styles it becomes especially important to promote effective communication and build respectful relationships.

Actively listening without assumptions using clear language and adapting communication styles that take account of factors such as that for some partners they may struggle with English (the usual operational language within a consortium), or cultural differences of expression in language and behaviours need to be considered and broadly accommodated. Therefore, not only be aware of direct communication but also be for non-verbal cues that may need management during information sharing meetings.

In a dynamic project environment, roles may need adjusting based on changing circumstances and requirements without compromising the integrity of the project structures. In such circumstances, it is essential to recognise the significance of the team leader in multidisciplinary teams as they play a role in both coordinating the project and managing interpersonal relationships within a team.

Therefore, you as project co-ordinator, and those team leaders within each work package need to project positive values and behaviours in relation to open communication style, accessibility, considerate to people's needs, and cognisant in supporting them when they encounter problems and adaptable problem solving. Above all, we have found that team leaders with a sense of humour often create a team milieu that is positive towards and engaged with the project work agenda, motivated and produce high quality outcomes.

To support the growth and development of your team members you should provide them with opportunities for learning, advancement, and skill building, such as training and mentorship in cognate skills that they don't possess but which may be useful to them in implementing the project. As part of this ensure you acknowledge and celebrate partner organisation and individual achievement, both within the project and successes outside of the project parameters.

Whenever possible it is beneficial to incorporate both, in-person and virtual team building exercises or activities. This builds trust among team members. Promote structured discussions that blend with social interactions. By including these gatherings in your face-to-face meetings agenda from the beginning of the project, you can establish an atmosphere that encourages discussions and fosters strong interpersonal relationships.

Finally, promoting an environment that promotes a work–life balance will contribute towards maintaining a positive team dynamic. Emphasise the importance of work practices such as no obligation to send or respond to communications that extend beyond normal working hours—usually within EU countries, this in 9 am to 5 pm. Don't hold meetings that breach these parameters, and when setting meetings up, remember to be aware of time differences between partner countries. For example, 1 pm in Ireland is 2 pm in Germany and 3 pm in Latvia.

To summarise, by nurturing such an environment, project co-ordinators and partners can enhance their team's effectiveness satisfaction levels and resilience.

## 5.8 Conclusion

In this chapter we described and discussed the most significant activities you need to engage with once your project has formally started. The 'Kick Off' meeting is essential in setting the environment and tone between consortium partners' relationships and commitment to the project processes. As such, for you, as project co-ordinator, there is a heavy responsibility to ensure an overall positive but 'business-like' atmosphere. There is a performative element in this—that is you need to project yourself as self-assured about the project's importance and the participatory significance of each of your partners in achieving success. Engaging partners with the development of the project manual and boards will make them feel valued as well as establishing the operational mechanisms. Get this initial stage of the project start up right and your consortium will bond and work well together over the trajectory of your project.

**C.-Andreas Dalluege** Founder and Managing Partner of IBK Group; Chairman of the European Business Excellence Network e.V.; National Council Member of the Irish Work Study Institute. Certified Advisor & Trainer of EFQM, Operating Partner and Trainer of Initiative Ludwig-Erhard-Preis (ILEP).

Since 1990 he participated as the senior researcher for his organisation in over 35 EU projects in most programme types offered by the EU and represented his company in all of them at the Management Board level as well as worked as our lead researcher in them.

He serves on the national board of the Irish Work Study Institute (IIESMS) and as President of the European Business Excellence Network (EuroBEN).

As a lecturer at the TH Aschaffenburg, he also gives classes on the design, proposing, and running of EU Research projects since 2019. Contact: cad@ibk.eu

**John Stephen Gary Wells** PhD, FAAN, FNMFRCSI (Ad Eundem) is Dean of the School of Health Sciences at the South East Technological University. John graduated from the University of Manchester with a degree in history. Following graduation, he trained and practised as a mental health nurse in London, eventually managing one of the busiest acute psychiatric admission units in the capital. John then transitioned from a clinical practice role to an academic one in 1993, moving to Ireland in 1998 to take up an academic position there.

John is an active and experienced researcher. As either Principal Investigator or co-investigator he has won funding from national and EU-funded research programmes to the value of 12 million Euros. He is a member of the National Research Ethics Committee for Clinical Trials in Ireland and holds visiting professorships at UCD, Ireland, King's College London, UK, and Maribor University, Slovenia. John has published 115 peer-reviewed papers, 7 technical reports (commissioned by regional, national, and EU agencies), 9 book chapters, and 1 book.

At the time of publication he is principal investigator for an EU4Health-funded project on enhancing the digital skills of the pan-European health care workforce. He is also chairperson of a COST Action on expanding the access of people with intellectual disabilities to cancer services. Contact: john.wells@setu.ie

# Chapter 6
# Implementing the Project

**C.-Andreas Dalluege, Kasandra Musović, and John Stephen Gary Wells**

Implementing a project funded by the European Union (EU) is an undertaking that entails translating project plans into steps, managing resources coordinating various activities, and navigating through challenges. In this chapter, we describe in further detail some of the approaches to implementation that we have only lightly touched on or not yet covered in the previous chapters.

## 6.1 Implementing English as the Shared Project Language

English is the Common Language for projects in terms of management and in reporting within EU projects. Despite Brexit, it has retained its position within the EU as the lingua franca between member states. This makes sense, as it is the most widely spoken second language across Europe.

Within our project experience, having participants within a consortium who either have poor command of English, have very heavy accents that mean it is not spoken clearly, or do not speak it at all is a significant challenge when progressing project aims. Therefore, you need to think very carefully indeed about including

C.-A Dalluege (✉)
IBK, Wiesbaden, Germany
e-mail: cad@ibk.eu

K. Musović
University Maribor, Maribor, Slovenia
e-mail: kasandra.musovic1@um.si

J. S. G. Wells
South East Technological University, Waterford, Ireland
e-mail: john.wells@setu.ie



C.-A. Dalluege, J. S. G. Wells (eds.), *Navigating an EU Research Project*, Management for Professionals, https://doi.org/10.1007/978-3-031-70928-9_6

participants who have poor to no skills in the speaking and writing of English. In this context, we highlight some issues you need to consider in this regard.

- **Language Proficiency**: Language proficiency in English needs to be handled with sensitivity. If a consortium partner includes members with little to no proficiency, we would advise you as project co-ordinator on a one-to-one basis to speak with the English proficient member of that consortium about your concerns early on. Ask them as to how they propose to manage the lack of proficiency. You should do this early in the project life cycle. If not, you may find, as we did in one project, that it becomes a significant hindrance when engaging with a partner to progress project work.
- **Cultural Sensitivity:** It's important to note that language usage is closely intertwined with culture. Thus, it is important to use plain as opposed to overly complex or ambiguous English phrases (particularly if you are a native speaker) to avoid misunderstandings. Avoid using jargon when explaining concepts and confirm understanding with partners to ensure messages are understood.
- **Awareness of linguistic misunderstanding due to differences in pronunciation, ambiguities, and accents:** Each country has its own version of English with a mix of accents, idioms, and local flavours that you will find reflected amongst the different partners in an EU project. This can lead to real difficulties in understanding, particularly ion online meetings where you may be denied body language cues that often indicate meaning in relation to speech. You might find yourself nodding along pretending to understand when in fact you do not. It is better to ask for clarification from the speaker, ask them to speak more slowly or ask them to use less jargon rather than leave a conversation without knowing/understanding its content.
- If you are anxious about raising this as an issue, use self-deprecating humour to highlight that you do not understand what was said. Such opportunities for laughter and occasional language mix-ups can turn into shared stories that can facilitate language clarity whilst avoiding insult. Remember it's hard speaking in foreign language and the effort to do so should be supported positively.
- **Implement your project communication strategy:** Implement your internal communication strategy. Make sure it emphasises cultural awareness and sensitivity in its communication protocols and that it encourages open dialogue among team members. Regular team meetings, cultural training sessions between members, and outline how those members with less optimal English will be supported.

## 6.2 Adapting the Project Instruments

Designing the instruments for your project, which include the tools, mechanisms to achieve your project's goals encompass elements, like research frameworks data collection tools, communication channels, collaboration platforms, monitoring, and evaluation frameworks. In this section we will provide an overview of considerations and best practices for designing project instruments.

The initial step in designing project instruments involves understanding the objectives and requirements of the project.

- What are the goals that need to be accomplished?
- What tasks must be undertaken to achieve these goals?
- Who are the stakeholders involved in the project?
- What resources are available for implementation?

By addressing these questions, one can better guide the design process for developing project instruments. You will largely have addressed these general design principles in the initial proposal. However, once your project has begun translating these principles and tools needs to be operationalised. Below we suggest some key instruments that are likely to feature within your project:

- **Data collection instruments**: Most projects incorporate data collection and analysis; Depending on your project's requirements there might be a need to create data collection tools such as surveys, interviews guides, or observation protocols, in order to gather information. These should be developed with reference to an overall research methodology. This is important as it protects your project from criticism that it is a-theoretical and therefore has limited validity in relation to the questions or issues it is trying to address. It often surprises us how neglected this aspect of data.

- The design of the tools you use should allow for the collection of valid data. It is important to pilot test and refine these tools. We have seen projects that have failed to consider how time-consuming piloting can be and has suffered in terms of criticism as a result. So ensure that you incorporate this aspect into your time lines for development.
- **Project website:** For most, though not all, EU-funded programmes there is an expectation that you deliver a project website to disseminate your project's progress. Make sure you cost the effort involved to both develop the website and maintain it over the course of your project. Look at its sustainable potential beyond the project's lifetime (see, for example, SSTeMM website which can be found at www.sstemm.eu and http://www.ibk.eu/en/products.php)
- A project website at a minimum will provide a description of your project, the organisations involved, how to contact the project team, and a regularly updated news section detailing project events and activities carried out by the consortium team. We also include links to YouTube videos that we make, links to tools that we develop (for example survey instruments), and articles that we have either published or have been produced by others that may be relevant to our project.
- **Collaboration platforms and archiving**: As we have indicated platforms such as MS Teams, Google Docs, or Dropbox (to name the most commonly used but not the only ones) are very useful in the facilitation of concurrent remote working between partners in the consortium. Before you choose which one to use, it is

important to assess your project's requirements for document sharing, task management, scheduling, video conferencing, and other collaborative activities and security levels. You also need to check with partners whether their respective institutions online firewall protections allow access to the chosen platform.

Once the consortium has agreed the platform, we strongly suggest you to hold some online collective training activities for your partners so that the individuals within your partnership are all operating at a minimum level of competence. This can save problems later. For example, in one project we led our failure to provide such training and assumption that all individuals within our consortium knew how to use our chosen collaborative platform resulted in one individual accidently deleting files that could not be retrieved.

The collaborative platform provides a collective approach for checking and archiving content-related progress across the consortium and saves time in gathering records required by the EU Project Office should they request them. To achieve this goal, you should design monitoring and evaluation framework (outlined in your original proposal) to include performance indicators (KPIs) methods for data collection well, as reporting procedures.

As part of the framework, implement a concise Monthly Status Report (MSR) that combines resource tracking (from time sheets) with content monitoring. Figure 6.1 provides an example of how you can structure such a report template.

- **Capacity Tools:** Depending on your project's objectives, it may be necessary to develop capacity tools like training materials, workshops, or mentoring programmes. Incorporate into your timeline sufficient capacity for their development as well as their testing and final implementation. Remember, because you are dealing with a pan-European profile you need to provide these tools in more than one language. It's important, therefore, that you account for the translation costs in your planning. In addition to English, we usually translate materials into all the languages of the respective participating partners.
- **Engagement channels:** Create strategies for stakeholders who are not part of consortium that raise awareness of and encourage engagement with your project. Since such stakeholders are not obliged to engage with you, these strategies need to be persuasive and rewarding for stakeholders. Therefore, you need to plan and implement meaningful engagement whilst being adaptable to stakeholder preferences and requirements.

For example, within the SSTeMM project we held a series of online (and after lockdown ended) in-person training sessions for clinicians and educators on how to manage their own stress and those of students. We also initiated several cost-free conferences where attendees received a certificate of attendance that they could use for their professional portfolio. Within DDS-MAP, we engaged with regulatory by providing them with a brief about current developments across Europe in relation to micro credentials in health services as a means of opening up engagement.

## 6.3 Language Translation, Testing, and Implementation of Project Instruments

Language translation, testing, and implementation involve a rigorous examination of the tools developed for your project and their subsequent deployment in the real world. This section will guide you through the intricacies of this process and provide tips to ensure its smooth execution.

- **Language translation of the instruments**: EU-funded projects are multi-lingual as they include partners drawn from countries across the EU and sometimes beyond. Whilst the operational language amongst consortium members will probably be English, the instruments you produce/deliver require, at a minimum, translation into the languages of target groups represented by the countries from where your partners come. As indicated above this can be time-consuming and you need to take account of this in your resource planning.

One of the major challenges is ensuring that meaning is not lost in cross translation. Thus, it is likely that your instrument first will be written in English, which then has to be translated into anything up to seven or more languages. Whilst there are commonalities between languages, not all words have equivalents in other languages or similar syntax.

When translating instruments, it is important to follow established guidelines and best practices to ensure across language groups translated versions' accuracy, validity, and reliability. We recommend you follow the guidelines below:

- **Professional Translation**: If your resources allow (dependent on the size of the grant you have been awarded), engage qualified professional translators fluent in both the source and target languages (they can be expensive so explore these costs prior to writing your proposal NOT once you have received funding). Translators should have a strong understanding of the research topic and terminology.

- If resources do not allow this type of sub-contracting, then explore with consortium partners whether they have people within their organisations with these skills to whom they can turn. There will still be a cost to this but it is likely to be cheaper than sub-contracting.
- **Maintain Conceptual Equivalence**: Focus on conveying the intended meaning and concepts rather than providing literal translations. Adapt the language to capture cultural nuances and ensure understanding in the target language. Focus on capturing the essence of what the instrument conveys without making your readers engage in a linguistic cognitive labour trying to decipher what you mean.
- **Collaborative Approach:** Work with a team of translators, subject matter experts, and cultural experts. Collaboration helps ensure accuracy and cultural sensitivity in translation, almost like forming a superhero team.
- **Back-Translation**: After translating the instrument, perform 'back-translation' by translating the translated version back into the source language. Compare the

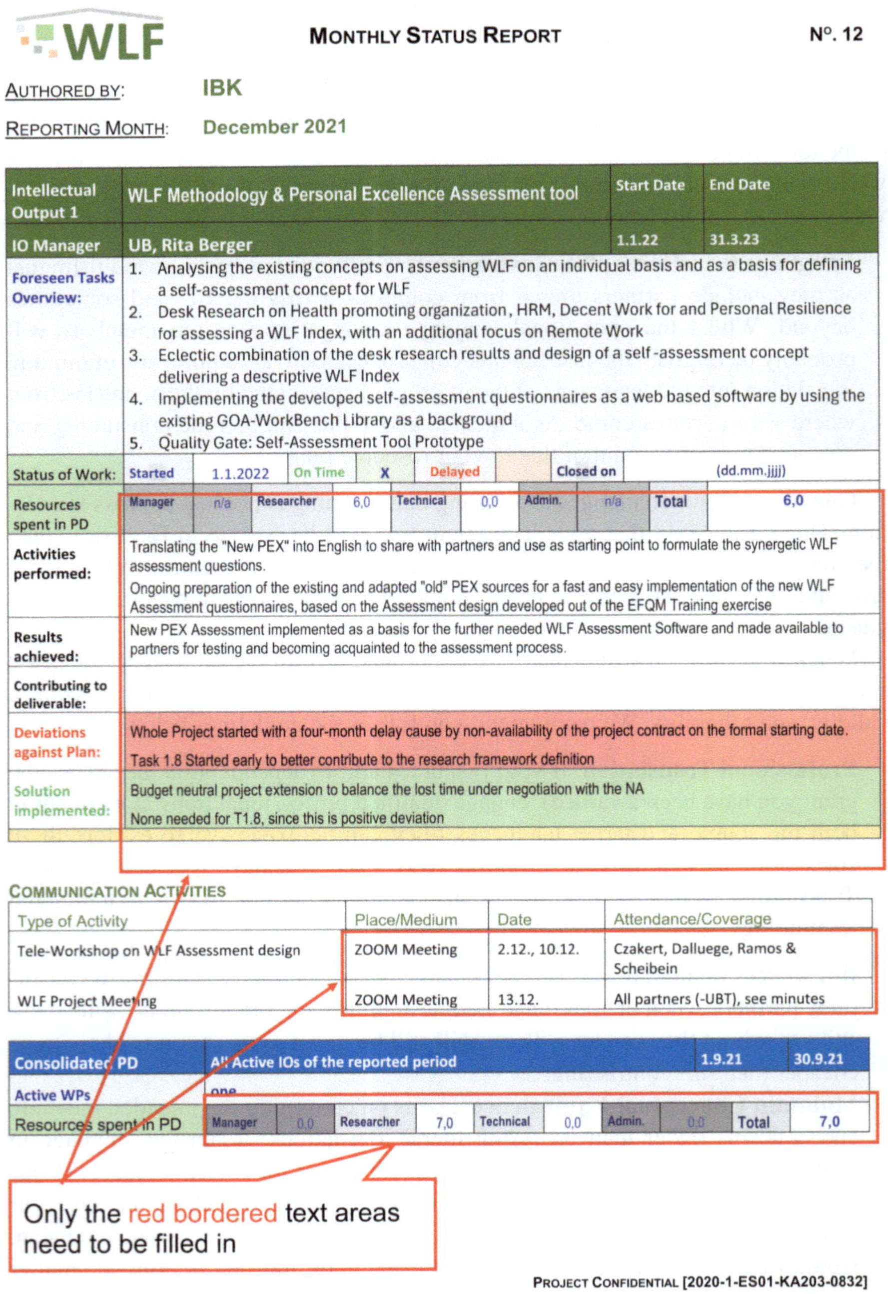

WLF **MONTHLY STATUS REPORT** **N°. 12**

AUTHORED BY: **IBK**

REPORTING MONTH: **December 2021**

| Intellectual Output 1 | WLF Methodology & Personal Excellence Assessment tool | Start Date | End Date |
|---|---|---|---|
| IO Manager | UB, Rita Berger | 1.1.22 | 31.3.23 |

**Foreseen Tasks Overview:**

1. Analysing the existing concepts on assessing WLF on an individual basis and as a basis for defining a self-assessment concept for WLF
2. Desk Research on Health promoting organization, HRM, Decent Work for and Personal Resilience for assessing a WLF Index, with an additional focus on Remote Work
3. Eclectic combination of the desk research results and design of a self-assessment concept delivering a descriptive WLF Index
4. Implementing the developed self-assessment questionnaires as a web based software by using the existing GOA-WorkBench Library as a background
5. Quality Gate: Self-Assessment Tool Prototype

| | | | | | | | | | |
|---|---|---|---|---|---|---|---|---|---|
| Status of Work: | Started | 1.1.2022 | On Time | X | Delayed | | Closed on | (dd.mm.jjjj) | |
| Resources spent in PD | Manager | n/a | Researcher | 6,0 | Technical | 0,0 | Admin. | n/a | Total 6,0 |

| | |
|---|---|
| Activities performed: | Translating the "New PEX" into English to share with partners and use as starting point to formulate the synergetic WLF assessment questions. Ongoing preparation of the existing and adapted "old" PEX sources for a fast and easy implementation of the new WLF Assessment questionnaires, based on the Assessment design developed out of the EFQM Training exercise |
| Results achieved: | New PEX Assessment implemented as a basis for the further needed WLF Assessment Software and made available to partners for testing and becoming acquainted to the assessment process. |
| Contributing to deliverable: | |
| Deviations against Plan: | Whole Project started with a four-month delay cause by non-availability of the project contract on the formal starting date. Task 1.8 Started early to better contribute to the research framework definition |
| Solution implemented: | Budget neutral project extension to balance the lost time under negotiation with the NA. None needed for T1.8, since this is positive deviation |

**COMMUNICATION ACTIVITIES**

| Type of Activity | Place/Medium | Date | Attendance/Coverage |
|---|---|---|---|
| Tele-Workshop on WLF Assessment design | ZOOM Meeting | 2.12., 10.12. | Czakert, Dalluege, Ramos & Scheibein |
| WLF Project Meeting | ZOOM Meeting | 13.12. | All partners (-UBT), see minutes |

| | | | | | | | | | | |
|---|---|---|---|---|---|---|---|---|---|---|
| Consolidated PD | All Active IOs of the reported period | | | | | | | 1.9.21 | 30.9.21 | |
| Active WPs | one | | | | | | | | | |
| Resources spent in PD | Manager | 0,0 | Researcher | 7,0 | Technical | 0,0 | Admin. | 0,0 | Total | 7,0 |



**Fig. 6.1** Example of MSR with minimised reporting effort per partner

back-translated version with the original to identify discrepancies and potential issues. If your words come back with a different meaning and/or emphasis, then explore how to correct this. Remember this is a complex activity since there may need to be cross referencing translation not just with the source language but also with the other languages in which the instrument is translated.

- **Pre-Testing**: Pre-test the translated instrument with a small sample from the target population. If they start scratching their heads in confusion, it might be time to rethink you're the translated instrument. Identify any issues related to comprehension, ambiguity, or cultural sensitivity.
- **Cognitive Interviews**: Conduct interviews with pre-test participants to understand how they interpret and respond to the translated questions to identify more nuanced issues with the translated instrument that may need correction.
- **Review and Iteration**: Review the translated instrument multiple times to ensure accuracy and clarity. Revise and refine the translation based on feedback and insights from experts and pre-testing.
- **Cultural Sensitivity**: When translating, consider cultural differences and sensitivities. Avoid questions or phrases that might be culturally inappropriate or offensive. Remember, what flies in one culture might crash and burn in another.
- **Maintain Documentation**: Keep detailed records of the translation process, decisions made, and any modifications. This documentation helps ensure transparency and reproducibility.
- **Piloting**: Pilot test the translated instrument on a larger sample from the target population. Assess the reliability and validity of the translated version.
- **Reporting**: Document the translation process in your research report or methodology section. Describe the steps taken to translate the instrument and address potential issues. This will significantly enhance the credibility of your findings with external audiences and assist in their adoption of your instruments for their own use or adopt recommendations you make in relation to the issue you are addressing.

In summary, remember that the translation process is a complex endeavour that requires careful attention to linguistic, cultural, and methodological factors. Adhering to these general guidelines will help ensure the translated research instrument maintains validity and accurately captures the intended information across different language groups. For more information on instrument development, translation, and testing, refer to Polit & Beck (2021) or Sousa & Rajjanasirat (2011) guidelines.

- **Testing the Project Instruments**: Apart from translation testing, it is important to test project instruments. Testing aims to identify and rectify any potential issues or gaps in your instrument in relation to what you want it to do (for example, in a survey, is it asking the right questions for the data you want to get). Depending on the nature of the instrument, testing could involve pilot studies, usability tests, or simulation.

- **Analysis of Testing Results**: Once the testing phase is complete, conduct a thorough analysis of the results. This analysis can reveal areas of strength and weakness within the project instruments and provide insights into how they might be improved. Be open to feedback and be prepared to make changes as necessary.
- **Refinement of Project Instruments**: Based on the analysis of the test results, you may need to refine or adjust your project instruments. This could involve minor or major changes. Remember, the goal is to create the most effective instrument for your project's success.
- **Training the Team**: It is crucial that all team members understand how to use the project instruments effectively. This may involve training sessions, workshops, or demonstrations. Make sure the team is comfortable with the instruments and can explain them and use them to their full potential.
- **Implementing the Project Instruments**: With testing complete, refinements made, and the team trained, it is time to implement the instruments to achieve the project's objectives. Carefully plan implementation. Generally, an instrument should be implemented at the same time by all relevant partners in the consortium. Sometimes, however, this is not possible so carefully document the reasons why this did not happen, consider whether it has had any impact on the results and how you mitigate any distortions as a result of not implementing the instrument at the same time. Implementation post launch carefully monitor its progress.
- **Monitoring and Evaluation**: On-going monitoring and evaluation allows you to track the effectiveness of the instruments and make any necessary adjustments. Regular check-ins, feedback sessions, and performance reviews by your consortium partners should take place and documented.
- **Dealing with Challenges**: Challenges that arise during the implementation phase are likely and need addressing quickly rather than avoided. This is where it is important to foster open communication within the consortium and foster, to coin an American phrase, a 'can do' approach. Avoid being 'problem paralysed', be 'solution focused'. In other words when a problem arises, articulate how to solve it to stimulate operational discussion between consortium partners.
- **Learning and Iteration**: The testing and implementation phase is an opportunity to gain insights about what works and what does not work. Then you adjust your instruments in response. This iterative process is a mark of success since nothing is perfect on 'a first try' basis. By showing how the instruments developed over time, you increase external stakeholders' confidence that they are reliable for use by them.

To summarise, by carefully allowing time to design your project instruments and recording changes made over the time of their implementation, you and your partners can enhance the project's effectiveness, efficiency, and sustainable impact with stakeholders.

## 6.4 Ethical Approval: Managing Different Processes, Different Demands, and Delays

When it comes to projects that involve data collection obtaining ethical approval is a significant aspect, which is often forgotten in timeline planning. In today's sensitive and legal climate of the rights of people to be fully informed, personal data protection, and penalties for research misconduct, you would be unwise not to obtain ethical approval.

You may have to obtain ethical approval from more than one organisation and across EU jurisdictions. Whilst ethical approval bodies generally operate to the same ethical principles, approval processes and local legislative requirements can lead to considerable delays in your project. In the following section, we explore the intricacies of this process and provide guidance on managing potential challenges.

### *6.4.1 Understanding Ethical Approval*

Ethical approval from a recognised approver, such as a university or health authority, serves as an assurance that research is in accordance with established standards and guidelines. Ethical approval entails a commitment on your part to follow principles and procedures when conducting studies involving people, animals, activity with an environmental impact that safeguard the well-being, rights, and dignity of all individuals involved in a study.

Approval also serves to protect you and your consortium from potential legal impacts by demonstrating that participants gave fully informed consent to take part in the research process. It demonstrates your commitment to being ethical in what you do.

At the core of research ethics is ensuring that people who agree to take part in your research are fully informed about what your research is about, what is expected of them, and what you will do with their data once given to you. As such, you, as the researcher, have a responsibility to provide information about your research that is plainly written and provides people with opportunities to seek clarifications. This includes explaining the purpose of your research, outlining the procedures involved, and discussing risks and benefits. You must also demonstrate that people have agreed to participate willingly without any form of coercion either directly from you or through a third party with whom you are associated—for example, a service manager supports your project and puts pressure on those who work in the service to participate.

Ethical approval requires an assessment of all risks associated with the research. This assessment includes evaluating social and other harms that participants or society may face. Researchers must take steps to minimise or address these risks effectively.

Confidentiality and privacy play a role in any research endeavour. You have an obligation to protect participants' sensitive/personal information and ensure that their identities remain undisclosed (anonymous, that is no one can link their data to their identity—including you), unless they give consent for this information to be released (either pseudo-anonymised—that is you know their identity—open—everyone knows their identity). When thinking about confidentiality, it is crucial for you to culturally interact with participants in a way that aligns with their context. You need to be mindful of the subtleties, within each country's culture to avoid any misunderstandings or ethical dilemmas.

### *6.4.2 Ethical Approval Committees and Different Jurisdictions*

As mentioned in the introduction to this section, to ensure compliance, with standards many institutions have established ethics committees or review boards. These bodies thoroughly evaluate research proposals to ensure they meet all ethical and legal requirements for the conduct of research. Without their approval, in many jurisdictions, such as Ireland, certain types of research, for example in the field of healthcare, are not legally protected.

Typically, these committees consist of experts from fields such as ethics, health care, social sciences, and law. The objective is to guarantee institutional compliance when conducting research involving subjects, animals, or the environment, referenced to institutional policies, national and international law, and principles of good research practice.

Bearing in mind that you are likely to need ethical approval from more than one jurisdiction, you, as project co-ordinator, will need to consider different demands in relation to submission content and time lines taken to obtain approval. This means understanding and adhering to each country's ethical frameworks and guidelines while overcoming language barriers and cultural differences. In this endeavour, you should be guided by the advice of your partners in the consortium. They will be best acquainted with local conditions. If you are wise, you will let them manage the submission within their local jurisdiction. Your role will be to co-ordinate these submissions across jurisdictions and hope approval can be obtained by an agreed time line end point.

Despite these challenges, obtaining approvals from countries through a process offers numerous benefits that greatly enhance the integrity and impact of the research. Thorough ethical scrutiny from different national jurisdictions ultimately improves the quality and credibility of the study and gives added credibility to its pan-European profile in terms of results. In this section we will explore strategies for navigating through this process.

- **Start Early**: It is advisable to initiate the approval ethical approval process early in the lifecycle of your project in order to account for any potential delays.

- **Understand Requirements:** Take some time to familiarise yourself with local guidelines and requirements set forth by the ethics committee.
- **Prepare a Comprehensive Application**: Ensure that your application within the supplied ethical form thoroughly addresses all aspects of your research.
- **Stay engaged with the Ethics Committee throughout the process**: Maintain lines of communication. Be prepared to address any questions they may have. Make sure your communications project a positive attitude to the process reflected in your willingness to accept critical review and revise your application accordingly.

As we have indicated, whilst specific procedures in obtaining ethical approval may vary depending on factors such as institutions, countries involved, and types of research conducted, below we lay out the general steps involved in submission and ethical review:

- **Submission of Research Proposal**: Researchers initiate the process by submitting a research proposal to an ethics review board or committee. This proposal includes details, about research goals, methodologies employed, participant recruitment strategies, data collection procedures, data analysis methods employed, as measures taken for data storage and security. It is crucial to outline your research plans comprehensively, starting from how you intend to identify participants through to how you plan to analyse their information.
- **Committee Review the research proposal:** The ethics committee reviews the proposal to ensure that it meets the standards and guidelines set by the institution and regulatory bodies.
- **Review of consent:** The committee will review your processes and information you provide to participants to obtain consent. You need to explain the purpose of the study procedures involved, potential risks and benefits, confidentiality measures, and participants' right to withdraw from the research and whether there are time limits beyond which they cannot withdraw. It's like inviting someone to dance. The ethics committee reviews the consent form to ensure it is easy for participants to understand and provides all information.
- **Laying out potential risks**: You need to highlight to the committee the balance between potential risks and benefits associated with your research, and how you will manage these. The ethics committee examines these assessments to make sure that potential benefits outweigh any risks involved and that you protect participants' well-being.
- **Confidentiality and data management:** The ethics committee is responsible, for reviewing protocols related to data management to ensure the privacy of participants and secure storage of data. The committee reviews your proposal as to how you manage and safeguard participants' personal information and who will have access to data and at what level. Who and what data will be accessed must be kept to a justified minimum.
- **Recruitment to your study:** The committee will examine who you proposed to recruit to the study and how they will be recruited. When it comes to recruitment, it is essential to demonstrate that your procedures avoid a favouritism, biases,

pecuniary incentive—especially in relation to vulnerable populations—or coercion. The ethics committee carefully examines recruitment strategies to prevent exploitation of populations.

- **Instruments and interventions:** For research instruments such as surveys, questionnaires or other tools or a proposed intervention, for example information giving about a health problem, the ethics committee assesses sensitivity, respectfulness, and potential impact on participants' well-being. The goal is to ensure that these instruments do not cause harm or distress.
- **Evaluation of conflicts of interest:** Researchers and institutions are obligated to disclose any conflicts that could influence the outcomes of their study. The ethics committee examines these disclosures with the aim of assessing whether they could compromise the study's integrity.
- **Ethical oversight over the course of research:** The ethics committee may require researchers to provide updates on the progress of their study. This allows for identification and resolution of any ethical issues that may arise during the research process. Such careful oversight ensures that research adheres to standards and avoids any misconduct. In cases of long-term studies, the ethics committee may require assessments to ensure that the research consistently adheres to standards and that any emerging ethical issues are reported with proposals for mitigation. The committee will also require that you seek permission from it prior to making any changes to the approved research protocol.

Ultimately, final approval from the ethics committee is necessary, before proceeding with the research project. After addressing any concerns raised by the ethics committee and making required revisions to the protocol researchers you will be granted approval to proceed with your research.

To summarise, whilst it can be challenging ultimately the ethical approval process enhances the quality and credibility of your project. It also serves to protect you and the consortium in the research process as well as participants. However, remember that ethical considerations go beyond obtaining approval. It is crucial that you and your consortium partners uphold standards at every stage of the project from recruiting participants and collecting data all the way through analysing and disseminating the results.

## 6.5 Conclusion

In this chapter, we provided in-depth description on how to implement your project and navigate some of the challenges that can arise. In particular, we focused on issues that, in our experience, project consortia either do not take into account when resource and timeline planning or allocate insufficient time and resources. In particular, we highlighted language translation, instrument design and testing, and ethical approval.

Bearing in mind how these three areas can be crucial within an EU-funded project it is curious that often in terms of resourcing and timelines they are neglected. Yet, these issues are easily foreseeable. By careful timeline planning and allocating sufficient resources in relation to that timeline consortium partnerships and you, as the project co-ordinator, can avoid many challenges and stressors associated with these key areas in the implementation process of your project. In the next chapter we look at less foreseeable and how to manage these.

**C.-Andreas Dalluege** Founder and Managing Partner of IBK Group; Chairman of the European Business Excellence Network e.V.; National Council Member of the Irish Work Study Institute. Certified Advisor & Trainer of EFQM, Operating Partner and Trainer of Initiative Ludwig-Erhard-Preis (ILEP). Since 1990 he participated as the senior researcher for his organisation in over 35 EU projects in most programme types offered by the EU and represented his company in all of them at the Management Board level as well as worked as our lead researcher in them.

He serves on the national board of the Irish Work Study Institute (IIESMS) and as President of the European Business Excellence Network (EuroBEN).

As a lecturer at the TH Aschaffenburg, he also gives classes on the design, proposing, and running of EU Research projects since 2019. Contact: cad@ibk.eu

**Kasandra Musović** Ph.D. cand. and registered nurse, since 2019 academic nurse and researcher with primary research areas are in the science of caring and nursing education. She has worked on several projects: Student Stress Training e-Mobile Management (SSTeMM) and Erasmus Mundus Design Measures (EMDM): Design and Implementation of Master Degree in Palliative Care (DSGN-PALL-CARE); and is currently working on EU4Health project The Dynamic Digital skills for Medical and Allied Professions in Health Services (DDS-MAP). She is also a student member of the European Academy of Nursing Science and the International Association of Human Caring and International Exchange Alumni, Bureau of Educational and Cultural Affairs. Contact: kasandra.musovic1@um.si

**John Stephen Gary Wells** PhD, FAAN, FNMFRCSI (Ad Eundem) is Dean of the School of Health Sciences at the South East Technological University. John graduated from the University of Manchester with a degree in history. Following graduation, he trained and practised as a mental health nurse in London, eventually managing one of the busiest acute psychiatric admission units in the capital. John then transitioned from a clinical practice role to an academic one in 1993, moving to Ireland in 1998 to take up an academic position there.

John is an active and experienced researcher. As either Principal Investigator or co-investigator he has won funding from national and EU-funded research programmes to the value of 12 million Euros. He is a member of the National Research Ethics Committee for Clinical Trials in Ireland and holds visiting professorships at UCD, Ireland, King's College London, UK, and Maribor University, Slovenia. John has published 115 peer-reviewed papers, 7 technical reports (commissioned by regional, national, and EU agencies), 9 book chapters, and 1 book.

At the time of publication he is principal investigator for an EU4Health-funded project on enhancing the digital skills of the pan-European health care workforce. He is also chairperson of a COST Action on expanding the access of people with intellectual disabilities to cancer services. Contact: john.wells@setu.ie

# Chapter 7
# Managing the Unforeseen Risk: The COVID-19 'Lockdown' and the SSTeMM Project

**Florian Scheibein and John Stephen Gary Wells**

Every project is susceptible to events that can lead to delays. Understanding how to manage these is important to maintain project momentum and achieve successful outcomes. As we have indicated there are events that have a risk of delaying your project implementation you can predict and manage (for example, one can predict that if your project requires ethical approval from one or more institutions this is likely to insert some delay and therefore needs to be accounted for in your timeline planning).

But, what about unforeseen events that lead to delays? These are minor usually and managed through small adjustments to work planning or reallocating tasks within your consortium. There are, however, some unforeseen events, that are so completely out of your control that they threaten your ability to achieve the promised outcomes. We experienced one such event—the COVID-19 pandemic and concurrent 'lockdown' in relation to the Student Stress Training e-Mobile Management (SSTeMM) project funded under Erasmus Plus programme. In this chapter, we share these experiences and how we managed them.

## 7.1 The Student Stress Training e-Mobile Management (SSTeMM) Project

The Student Stress Training e-Mobile Management (SSTeMM) project was a three-year project funded under the Erasmus Plus programme. The consortium involved three higher education institutions (HEI)—the Waterford Institute of Technology in

F. Scheibein · J. S. G. Wells (✉)
South East Technological University, Waterford, Ireland
e-mail: Florian.Scheibein@setu.ie; john.wells@setu.ie



C.-A. Dalluege, J. S. G. Wells (eds.), *Navigating an EU Research Project*, Management for Professionals, https://doi.org/10.1007/978-3-031-70928-9_7

Ireland (now the South East Technological University)—the coordinator of the project; The University of Maribor in Slovenia and the TecnoCampus University in Spain. In addition, there were two non-HEI partners—the University of Pittsburgh Medical Centre (UPMC) Whitfield Hospital in Ireland and IBK Management Solutions in Germany.

The aim of the SSTeMM project was to develop an end-user (which was defined as a student nurse, the hosting clinical institution and HEI clinical support staff) accessible digital mobile platform of targeted work-based education, competency training and in vivo self-reflection learning opportunities. These would equip students and mentoring workers with the knowledge, skills and competencies to address occupational stressors (both personal and environmental). The focus was on a pedagogy that develops personal skills to build resilience that supports student and post qualifying retention within the workforce.

It took as its policy justification the integration of EU policy with WHO policy. EU policy was the European Pact on Mental Health (2008). This called for educational institutions to 'implement mental health and well-being programmes with risk assessment and prevention programmes for situations that can cause adverse effects on the mental health of workers'. In the proposal we argued that this policy integrated with the World Health Organisation's concept of the Health Promoting University (1998). The SSTeMM project could act as an operational case exemplar of such integration. In addition, we argued that the project outcomes could be generalised to the wider EU workforce in support of the aims of the European Agency for Safety and Health at Work.

To demonstrate the credibility of members of the consortium in this field three previously completed EU-funded projects were cited in which we were involved. The first was the Reducing Occupational Stress in Employment (ROSE) project. This developed an online supportive stress management training for health and social care workers (completed in 2010).

The second was the Developing E-Learning Accreditation to Reduce Occupational Stress in Employment (DELAROSE). This established a level 6 ECTS online accreditation framework for health and social care workers who completed a programme of training in the management of stress in the workplace (completed in 2015).

Finally, the improving management competences on excellence-based stress avoidance and working towards sustainable organisational development in Europe (IMPRESS). This developed tools and modules on 'work-related stress' issues so that health and social care organisations can recognise stress potentials in the organisation that facilitate staff training to prevent employee stress. This project was completed in 2019.

To justify the need for a trans-national EU project in this field the application highlighted that nursing is one of the most mobile regulated professions in terms of workforce movement across Europe. It is also regulated at both national and EU level in terms of equivalency recognition of training and licence to practice between EU states. As such, we argued that a pan-European co-operation would be both warranted and desirable and would translate into both European and national domains in terms of curricula change.

Based on the above the consortium funding for three years was awarded. The project 'kick off' launch took place in Dublin in September 2019. SSTeMM was completed in August 2023. As the completion timeline indicates it ran over its original timeline by a year. It is the reasons for that timeline over run and how it was managed that we address in the next section.

## 7.2 The COVID Lockdown and Uncertainty

Following the 'kick off' the consortium proceeded to implement the work package activities as outlined in the now funded application. The first activities were to develop a survey instrument about nursing stress to be administered to the target groups online to be followed by focus groups to explore with the target groups to explore the survey results and a user consultation on their experience of using the mobile application once it was developed and piloted. The second concurrent activity was to obtain ethical approval for the implementation of the above research-related activities from the ethics committees of the participating HEIs within the consortium.

There was marginal slippage in the translation timelines for the survey instrument for cross translation between English, Spanish, Slovenian and German of about six weeks. This had a 'knock on' effect in the submission for ethical approval from the HEI ethics committees. However, all ethical approvals were complete by February 2020. The consortium was now ready to engage with the target groups in relation to the survey instrument and the follow-up activities (other elements of the project were completely on time such as developing the background technological requirements to implement the mobile application once we had finalised content).

As we were progressing the project the new coronavirus (SARS-CoV-2 or Covid 19) affecting the population of the city of Wuhan in China started to appear in the media in December 2019. To be honest we paid little to no attention to the potential impact of the virus on the project (this despite reports between January and March 2020 of its progress across the world). The first time we realised its potential impact was following the worldwide pandemic declaration on March 11, 2020, by the World Health Organisation. A week later, everyone of our respective governments had declared a national lockdown.

The COVID-19 lockdowns, travel restrictions and other policy changes (for example, physical distancing restrictions) severely affected the project introducing significant uncertainty. One of the key elements in relation to this uncertainty was that we were engaged with sector that was most 'frontline' affected by COVID—namely, the health services and specifically nurses. Thus, within a month of lockdown as the cases rose and the hospitals became full, our primary target group, both qualified nurses and student nurses, became drawn into managing the challenges placed on health services and away from what would be their normal duty of mentoring and clinical teaching and being a learner and a student nurse. For example, in Ireland in April 2020 all fourth-year student nurses were called upon to help manage the crisis whilst student nurses from years 1 to 3 were asked to volunteer as nursing aides. The response was tremendous, but it meant the raison d'etre of STeMM was completely disrupted.

## 7.3 Our Response

Many activities had to be paused. Others had to be stopped or completely rethought. Our first decision was that we had to move our planned in-person meeting (set for May in Spain) had to be online and postpone all in-person meetings indefinitely.

- **Initially Assessing the Impact**: This step involved evaluating how the lockdown might affect project timelines. This entailed reviewing each task of the project to identify likely delays caused by lockdown measures and estimating the time needed to complete the remaining work under these circumstances.
- It should be emphasised that we were dealing with a good deal of context uncertainty, which initially made these reviews more optimistic than subsequent events proved. None of us at this time had any idea how long 'lockdown' would last—broadly speaking we thought maybe a month or two. By the end of May 2020, we realised it that was not going to be the case. However, arising out of this exercise we realised we had to delay the recruitment of student nurses until it became clearer what the impact would be on them and second to re-evaluate our proposed dissemination activities (which had been envisioned as in-person activities).
- **Lesson learned**: The lesson we learned and then implemented from our initial assessment experience was that the unpredictable nature of the pandemic called for flexibility in terms of roles, tasks and expectations, within the project team. Consortium partners had to be prepared for an across task implementation and support approach that was not envisaged in the original project protocol. We were lucky in that all the collaborating partners knew each other very well based on previous collaborations (except for one) which facilitated this. However, the partner who was not well-known to the rest of the consortium tended to stick to its allocated role and was less flexible in taking on other tasks. Having said that they carried out their envisaged role impeccably.
- **Implementing the New Plan**: Once we established that a dynamic timeline needed to be implemented, we also looked at what we could achieve in relation to remote working and our target groups. We decided we could proceed with survey (which was an online activity) and advertise it to students through advertising its existence to students through the online routes that they often communicated through with their respective HEIS.
- We also decided that the other consultative tasks such as using Zoom, for dissemination to health care organisations and senior clinical and education manag-

ers would use if lockdown rules continued. We adapted our plans for mobile application development by deciding to rely on survey results and expertise within the group to develop content. Focus groups, which would be online, would purely look at the user experience.

- Our next task was to put these plans into action. This meant overseeing the project tasks according to the updated plan whilst acknowledging it would need to change as events unfold. This would therefore involve closely monitoring progress more than usual in project management.
- **Lesson learned:** The lesson we learned was the need to 'let go' to some extent of our learned preconceptions about how a project should be implemented. We all had considerable experience of project implementation; however, this was very much wedded to traditional concepts of 'doing research' and project development. We had to learn to let go of these traditional methods and approaches. This proved harder, from a personal psychological viewpoint, than one might think and demanded considerable discussion between consortium partners in terms of progressing the project in the 'new normal'.
- **On-going Evaluation:** Once we had agreed on our approach, continuous evaluation of the project' progress in each jurisdiction against time lines and unfolding events became a constant. This was necessary in that each jurisdiction—Ireland, Germany, Slovenia and Spain—had variance in both regulations but also on the demands/educational approaches, each jurisdiction was making in relation to our target groups.
- This involved regular check-ins at each online consortium meeting (which occurred every two weeks) to assess progress, identify any challenges that had emerged in any one jurisdiction and adjust as required. Whilst this may seem unproblematic at times, meetings could be tense as jurisdictional and, indeed, cultural differences came to the fore, particularly as many members had other work pressures arising from their respective organisations' response to the pandemic. Much of these challenges were associated with remote working.
- **The Transition to Remote Working:** A key feature of 'lockdown measures' was the sudden change to a remote working environment based on the internet. The first challenge this posed for the consortium was the variance in internet connectivity. Some members had fast broadband and others had very poor broadband.
- As a result, it was not unusual for members of the consortium falling out of online meetings because their broadband was so slow or 'freezing' for minutes whilst in the meeting. Email exchanges became an important mechanism in dealing with this situation but were by no means ideal and considerable stress and frustration could arise because of this 'internet poverty' within the consortium.
- In addition to internet poverty, many members of the consortium had to purchase new equipment (for example, second monitors, ergonomic chairs, headsets, etc.) as well as shop for new internet providers (and/or increase the speed of our current connections).
- All of us were isolated from people and society and we tried to support each other online as much as possible. One notable feature in terms of this support was how much time we spent talking about our hope for the return of in-person

meetings and in-person workshops. We did run over time several online workshops and dissemination events. They proved to be very unsatisfying as an experience and rather demoralising with many attendees leaving their cameras switched off. In fact, we noted at times that some attendees were not actually present but attending in name only.

- **Lesson learned:** We were, over time, acutely aware of the negative effect of the pandemic on ourselves. Stress at home and lack of social contact all played a part in this. We did our best to support one another through the online meetings (humour played a key role in alleviating tensions and communicating empathy to one another) but the stress of working in such a new environment took a toll on us all.
- **Contact with the National Agency/ National Contact Point:** When lockdown occurred it just so happened that the Irish National Agency/ National Contact Point (NCP) decided to conduct a review of projects they were funding at WIT/ SETU, including SSTeMM. Originally, this review was planned as an in-person visit but due to lockdown it became an online one. Thus, we had the opportunity early on in the pandemic to talk directly to the NCP senior management about our uncertainties, particularly in relation to timelines, and how we should manage these. The NCP recognised these challenges and provided reassurance that they were taking in consideration the lockdown disruption to projects.
- The pandemic changed how the NCP managed its projects. Our NCP regularly communicated changes to us and encouraged us to contact them in relation to challenges/ obstacles to the project. Through these discussions, the NCP offered to extend the timeline for project completion by one year. This came as a great relief to all the members of the consortium. They followed up on this extension with an offer of an additional six months of funding to support the project. Again, this came as a great relief in terms of institutional pressures placed on some members of the consortium.
- **Lesson learned:** Our interactions with the NCP highlighted how important engagement with them is when confronted with a completely unforeseeable event occurs. We found the Irish NCP to be very responsive and willing to engage in problem-solving. It should be noted that EU National Agencies/ NCP have to operate within rules set by the EU so sometimes they cannot be as responsively flexible as they might like. But this does not preclude them from giving advice as to how you might manage problems within the rules.
- One thing we should also point out about EU National Agencies is that they are culturally specific in their operating approach. Some of us were involved in other projects managed by NCPs in other jurisdictions. Some of these NCPs, reflective of their cultural norms, could be much more bureaucratic and less willing to engage in direct dialogue compared to the SSTeMM experience. Whilst outcomes were not dissimilar to the SSTeMM outcomes, the experience of 'getting there' was very different.

Sometimes external factors impact a project severely and need to be addressed to maintain reasonable results even though some of the original project objectives cannot be met any more due to factors completely outside the project's sphere of influence. In the case of SSTeMM such a factor was the COVID-19 pandemic which affected not only the operational aspects of the project but also the interpersonal dynamics within project's team. It highlighted the importance of empathy, open communication and adaptability in maintaining a cohesive and supportive team.

Based on our experience of SSTeMM during the 2020 'lockdown' we would emphasise that managing internal relations through regular virtual meetings, email updates and an open environment that facilitated discussions helped create a sense of unity among team members that in turn facilitated problem solving in a dynamic and uncertain operating environment. From our experience we would emphasise the following key messages.

Acknowledging the emotional impact of the pandemic on team members during these meetings was crucial. It facilitated a joint problem-solving approach that generally fostered a supportive work environment. Though at times the stress people were under broadly did at times lead to tensions between members.

Promoting well-being of team members by an understanding group culture in which humour and flexibility were key components in the management of tensions between partners. Where conflict arose, the focus was on finding solutions rather than placing blame thereby diffusing potential disruptive and bitter argument.

Adapting to changing circumstances was a key aspect of managing internal relations. This involved being flexible with roles and responsibilities, understanding individual constraints and adjusting expectations as needed.

A significant strategic element in supporting the team and promoting the project's progress was the relationship with the NCP. It's 'can do' attitude and willingness to engage directly with the SSTeMM team was key in both supporting the ultimate success of SSTeMM but also in supporting the well-being of the SSTeMM consortium members.

## 7.4 Conclusion

In conclusion, managing internal relations and promoting well-being were key aspects of navigating the project during the COVID-19 pandemic. Despite the challenges, these efforts helped maintain team unity, boost morale and ensure the continued progress of the project. We learned many useful lessons during COVID-19, some outlined in this chapter and others set out in Chap. 9 below. The overall experience underscored the importance of putting people first and communicating empathically, when in the midst of a crisis.

**Florian Scheibein** is a Research Assistant and PhD student at the School of Health Sciences, South East Technological University. He is currently the Lead Research Assistant for an EU4Health project—DDS-MAP—and Grant Holder Manager for an EU COST Action—CUPID. He has been involved in three ERASMUS projects and was the co-recipient of the Council of Europe Pompidou Group European Drug Prevention Prize for one of these projects. He is an Editor for the Harm

Reduction Journal and is a Co-Director and General Secretary of the Network of Early Career Professionals in Addiction Medicine which works with the World Health Organisation's Alcohol, Drugs and Addictive Behaviours Unit. Contact: Florian.Scheibein@setu.ie

**John Stephen Gary Wells** PhD, FAAN, FNMFRCSI (Ad Eundem) is Dean of the School of Health Sciences at the South East Technological University. John graduated from the University of Manchester with a degree in history. Following graduation, he trained and practised as a mental health nurse in London, eventually managing one of the busiest acute psychiatric admission units in the capital. John then transitioned from a clinical practice role to an academic one in 1993, moving to Ireland in 1998 to take up an academic position there.

John is an active and experienced researcher. As either Principal Investigator or co-investigator he has won funding from national and EU-funded research programmes to the value of 12 million Euros. He is a member of the National Research Ethics Committee for Clinical Trials in Ireland and holds visiting professorships at UCD, Ireland, King's College London, UK and Maribor University, Slovenia. John has published 115 peer-reviewed papers, 7 technical reports (commissioned by regional, national and EU agencies), 9 book chapters and 1 book.

At the time of publication he is principal investigator for an EU4Health-funded project on enhancing the digital skills of the pan-European health care workforce. He is also chairperson of a COST Action on expanding the access of people with intellectual disabilities to cancer services. Contact: john.wells@setu.ie

# Chapter 8
# Reporting and Promoting the Outcomes of Your Project to Stakeholders and Evaluators and Drafting the Final Report

**C.-Andreas Dalluege, Kasandra Musović, Florian Scheibein, Gregor Štiglic, and John Stephen Gary Wells**

A critical aspect of project management is the final report which articulates how you measured project outcomes against the predefined deliverables and how well you disseminated your project outcomes both at the time you were carrying out the project and post the funded lifetime of your project. As we previously indicated EU financial support for a project is based on achieving the key indicators as laid out in the original application. In this chapter we provide guidance on measuring your deliverables, how to promote and disseminate them and principles to be followed in drafting and submitting the final report.

C.-A Dalluege (✉)
IBK, Wiesbaden, Germany
e-mail: cad@ibk.eu

K. Musović
University Maribor, Maribor, Slovenia
e-mail: kasandra.musovic1@um.si

F. Scheibein
South East Technological University, Waterford, Ireland
e-mail: Florian.Scheibein@setu.ie

G. Štiglic
University Maribor, Maribor, Slovenia
e-mail: gregor.stiglic@um.si

J. S. G. Wells
South East Technological University, Waterford, Ireland
e-mail: john.wells@setu.ie


C.-A. Dalluege, J. S. G. Wells (eds.), *Navigating an EU Research Project*, Management for Professionals, https://doi.org/10.1007/978-3-031-70928-9_8

## 8.1 Measuring and Reporting on Key Project Indicators

In a project, evaluating outcomes based on the stated deliverables is one of the most important project activities in relation to reporting project success. It defines success for those you report to, that is your EU funders, your consortium partner organisations, those with whom you have consulted in your project and the wider audience with whom you wish to communicate. Below (and in Fig. 8.1) we outline some key components for this.

As a project progresses, however, goals not defined in the original application, but that arise based on individual partner interests as the project progresses, can divert and side track your project away from its original stated deliverables if not recognised and managed. This does not mean that these individual goals are not worth achieving as "value-added" outcomes; but as a co-ordinator, you must ensure that they do not become the focus of your achievement reporting at the expense of the original stated deliverables. Below we identify what you must do to demonstrate that you have achieved your project deliverables through your key indicators.

- **Defining Deliverables**: This step involves revisiting, on a regular basis, the project's outputs as stated in the project proposal and contract. Gather data on both the associated processes you implemented and evidence of achievement to communicate project fidelity to their achievement.
- **Monitoring and Reporting Performance Metrics**: Consistent monitoring of performance metrics against those stated in your funded application are crucial. These metrics are quantifiable and directly linked to the deliverables.
- You should collect data on these performance metrics during the project—don't neglect them, which can easily happen as the project progresses and you become distracted by day-to-day management issues. Analyse the data and compare it against the performance metrics. Make sure you report the analysis of performance

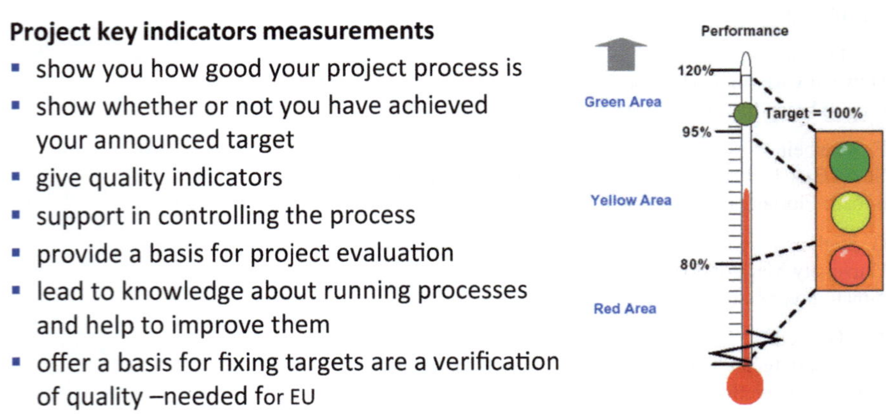


**Fig. 8.1** Measuring project KPI

metrics in the final report—remember it is most likely that English is a reviewer's second language so keep the narrative simple in order that this aspect can be clearly understood,

- **Reporting change**: Given that over the funded lifetime of a project events are likely to occur that may impact on deliverables. As described in the previous chapter some events may have highly significant impacts. It is, therefore, very important that you describe both the impacts and how you tried to manage them in relation to the intended deliverables. Sometimes such events make it impossible to deliver exactly what you promised in the original application for funding.
- Though you may be marked down by the evaluators in relation to this by showing what you did to mitigate the impacts in order to achieve as close as possible the promised deliverables you will not be penalised heavily. Therefore, keep copious records of changes, why they occurred and your rationale for project adjustments to mitigate impacts.

In conclusion, the process of evaluating and reporting outcomes against deliverables involves demonstrating robust performance metrics, and consistent monitoring practices and good recordkeeping linked to adaptability in managing project changes are key components in the effective reporting to funders.

## 8.2 Promoting Your Project and Maintaining Partnerships Post-Project Funding

Successfully promoting a project is crucial, for its success, visibility and impact. It goes beyond showcasing the project's objectives and outcomes during its funded lifetime. It also involves sourcing and contacting stakeholders, not just your consortium partners, who can contribute to its dissemination beyond it funded lifetime. This also means demonstrating longer lasting partnerships to support project impact beyond the funded lifetime of the project.

By doing this you will be able to point to a history of impact credibility for your future submissions for funding. This section explores the particulars involved in promoting your project, both during its timeline and post funded follow-up.

General Principles to follow

- **Identifying and making contact with target audiences:** From an early stage you need to identify specifically your target audience. This encompasses immediate beneficiaries, and direct and potential stakeholders who could both contribute to and benefit from the project's goals. Understanding this target audience is essential in the tailoring of your promotion strategy and should be stated in terms of specifics rather than generalities accompanied by timelines and purposes to make contact with these "external" (that is not your consortium partners) across the lifetime of the project.

- By highlighting and effectively communicating how the project offers advantages and benefits to the target audience your promotion efforts became more impactful and demonstrable in terms of your final report to the funders of your project.
- **Crafting Messages**: In engaging with the external audiences, it is important that your messaging (both written and verbal) show that your project processes and deliverables align with their values, beliefs and goals. As part of this engagement think about creating compelling messages that are bespoke relevant to each stakeholder. Thus, you should try and avoid generic messaging if possible.
- For each stakeholder communicate your project's goals, progress and impact in a way that will resonate with them.
- This can be achieved by personalised communication to specific contacts for each stakeholder through addressing them by name and acknowledging their interests or needs and how your project deliverables will specifically serve these. Remember to demonstrate how your project can add value to their lives or that of their organisation.
- This personal touch will generally make a favourable impression on external stakeholders. In reporting these communications and responses to them in your report to your funders you will demonstrate that your project's value proposition was relevant to different groups with distinct needs that were complementary to the deliverables and thereby highly likely to be taken up by these stakeholders post funding.
- For example, in the SSTeMM project we contacted educational institutions that trained student nurses, clinical services that hosted student nurses and organisations that were concerned with the broad mental health of students whilst in education. For all these groups we crafted messages that demonstrated how the SSTeMM project could support them.
- Thus, for educational institutions that trained nurses we highlighted the educational impact of the project in training nurses about the principles of stress management and deliverable that might support higher education institutions to prepare student nurses for their clinical placement. For clinical service we emphasised the support that the deliverables could give to registered nurses whilst mentoring student nurses whilst in their service, thereby reducing the stress on registered nurses when managing student nurses. For wider stakeholders we emphasised the potential of the project to be generalised to supporting other student groups who might have an extended employment placement as part of their course of study.
- **Using Communication Channels:** You need to think carefully about the appropriate communication channels to use in relation to your target audiences. Whilst most projects will require a website which provides general information about a project with possible supporting resources, this very much relies on an individual finding the website and landing on the page (see https://sstemm.eu/as an example of a website). A website, therefore, is a dissemination mechanism but not necessarily an effective way of promoting your project to stakeholders who know nothing about it.

– A website's real value (if it can be maintained) is that it is a tangible example of how you intend to maintain the project post funding. So, putting effort into its appearance and content is a mark of post funding credibility and impact in terms of reporting to the funding evaluators.
– Social media platforms, newsletters, press releases, public presentations and attending networking events can all be used to promote your project. But again, these will have different impacts for different audiences. For example, if your audience is a younger demographic Facebook is unlikely to be an effective communication channel compared to TikTok or Instagram. Therefore, think carefully about the channels most likely to reflect the interests of your stakeholders.
– For example, in the SSTeMM project we found that certain cases called for approaches like phone calls and face-to-face meetings to effectively reach our target audience. To enhance the effectiveness of our messaging we incorporated visual and multimedia elements such as infographics, videos and images within our website. We found that the more audio-visual rather than text reliant we were in our communication channels, the more effective we were.

### 8.2.1 Establishing Post-Project Cooperation

Maintaining a post-project cooperation structure that supports disseminating the project results to a wider public is important to demonstrate to evaluators in terms of impact beyond a project's final financing. Whilst a project's long-term success cannot be controlled by the funding authorities, the implementation of a credible, sufficient and sustainable cooperation support structure can be checked and will impact on the project's final evaluation.

A possible cooperation diagram is shown in Fig. 8.2 below.

For the post-project activities, it is important to pay attention to the open access conditions of many project strands. We spoke already on IPR and Foreground versus Background Materials in previous chapters but for the Dissemination and Exploitation Plan—which is a default deliverable in many programmes—this must be made more concrete.

A good way to balance the requirements of open access and proprietary results is given with the Creative Commons licensing approach. This will allow you to balance free access to end users with your own commercial interest for earning money to maintain and advance the project results.

Figure 8.3 below shows with the SSTeMM example how such a mix of freely available modules developed within the project can be interlinked with commercially sold interaction, based on the increasing commercial benefit to the end user organisation.

Keeping communication channels open during the pandemic "lock down"—our experience with the SSTeMM project and lessons learnt.

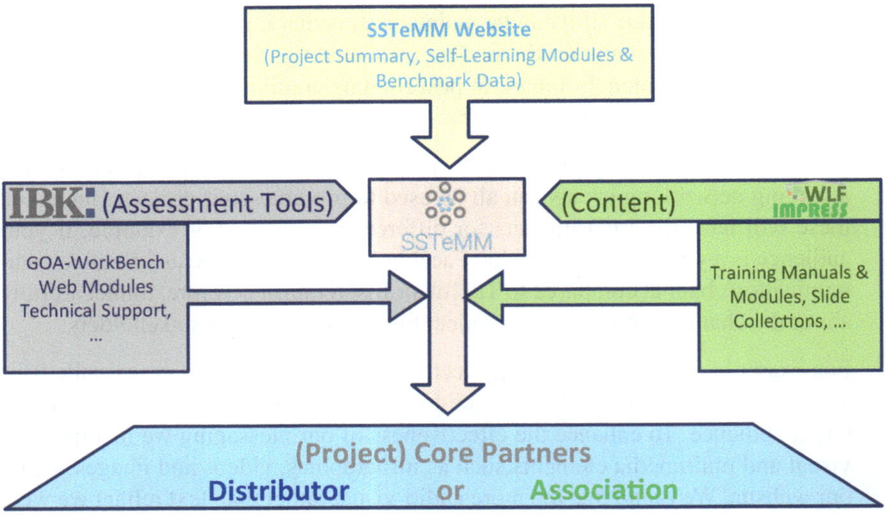


**Fig. 8.2** Post-project cooperation structure (example)

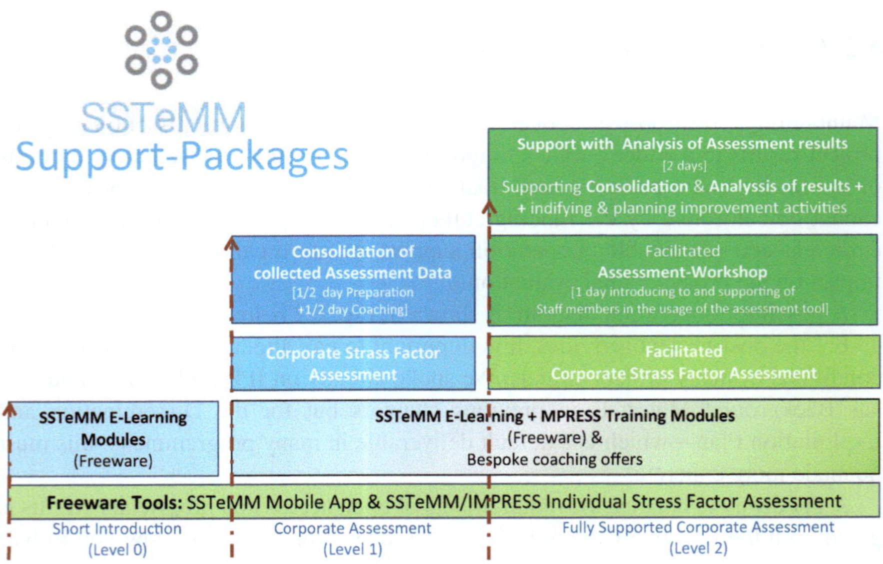


**Fig. 8.3** Post-project use of results achieved

Within the SSTeMM project, encouraging interaction and involvement of stakeholders became more difficult over the course of the pandemic lockdown which began across Europe from March 2020 and did not ease until October 2020. We had to find ways to engage stakeholders while adhering to related restrictions. We inevitably relied principally on virtual meetings with stakeholders and a series of online events. However, whilst this generally worked in raising awareness, they often felt impersonal compared to face-to- face interactions and in terms of online events (for example, training) we would often see cameras switched off and it became apparent that some attendees were there in name only—a somewhat demoralising experience for us!

Despite these challenges our promotional efforts led us to form partnerships. These partner stakeholders brought perspectives, resources and networks that enriched our project's impact. It was serendipitous that our project focused on stress management at a time when student nurses, registered nurses, academics and society more widely were experiencing significant stress. In this sense, SSTeMM was the right project for the predicament stakeholders were experiencing.

We made sure to align their expertise with the project's goals and assess their potential to make a contribution. It was important for the project to have strength that would actually improve people's lives.

To keep track of our communication and dissemination efforts we continuously evaluated them. This involved keeping a record of whether and the degree to which our communications engaged our audience through their immediate and follow-up responses to messaging. For example, we used tools to measure website traffic and interactions, on media, which helped us understand which platforms and messages resonated most with our target audiences. We also took the opportunity to encourage feedback questions and open dialogue with the groups we were targeting through providing project contact details and through direct dialogue in virtual meetings.

The experience of promoting the project taught us lessons. It emphasised the significance of understanding our target audience in depth and crafting messages utilising commonly used, as opposed to our preferred virtual channels.

The "lock down" underscored the significance of thinking in depth and strategically about not only what you want to promote but also the most effective and targeted communication channels to do that promotion.

## 8.3 What Was Delivered Beyond the Deliverables

While projects are typically evaluated based on the achievement of predefined deliverables, the true impact often extends beyond. The SSTeMM project was no exception, delivering value and impact that went beyond the specified deliverables. Beyond the deliverables, the project provided us with valuable lessons in project management, team dynamics, adaptability and resilience. This section outlines some of these extra outcomes:

- **Capacity Building:** Beyond achieving the deliverables, the project contributed significantly to capacity building among the team members and partners. They gained valuable skills and knowledge in project management, research and stress management, which they could apply in their future work.

- **Strengthened Partnerships:** The project also served to strengthen partnerships among the participating institutions. These relationships went beyond the life of the project, creating opportunities for future collaboration and shared learning.
- **Enhanced Visibility:** Through the promotional efforts, the project and the participating institutions gained enhanced visibility. This raised their profile and created opportunities for further funding and partnerships which have been followed up successfully in terms of awards such as the subsequent DDS-MAP project which is currently on-going.
- **Impact on external stakeholders:** The findings and recommendations from the project had an impact on implementation of stress management in education in some of the higher education institutions with which we made contact. This extended the project's influence beyond the partners within the project.
- **Personal Growth:** Team members experienced personal growth through their involvement in the project. This included improved communication skills, problem-solving abilities, adaptability and resilience, particularly in the face of the challenges posed by the COVID-19 pandemic.
- **Long-term Impact:** The project's impact extended beyond its duration. The tools and resources developed continue to be used (particularly the mobile application). Also, the project provided a good starting point to go for new EU Research proposals that build on the results achieved. In the case of the SSTeMM Project, these were the EU4Health project DDS-MAP and the ERASMUS+ Project Work-Life-Flow.

In conclusion, while the SSTeMM project successfully achieved its deliverables, it also delivered value and impact that went far beyond these. These additional outcomes underscore the broader impact of project work and the potential for projects to contribute to capacity building, relationship strengthening, policy influence, personal growth and long-term impact.

## 8.4 What Do Evaluators of Project Outcomes Look for?

Project evaluators play a significant role in determining the success and impact of a project. Evaluators have the responsibility of assessing whether the project has achieved its objectives, delivered expected results and provided value to stakeholders. In this section we outline the factors that evaluators typically consider when evaluating project outcomes.

- **Relevance:** Evaluators take into account how relevant the project is to the needs and priorities of the target group, stakeholders and overall context. They assess whether the objectives of the project align with identified needs, priorities and policies.
- **Effectiveness:** Evaluators analyse how well a project has achieved its goals and deliverables. They analyse the results, outputs and outcomes to determine if the project has successfully achieved its objectives and made the intended impact.

- **Efficiency:** Evaluators also assess how effectively resources such as time, money and personnel have been used to achieve the stated outcomes. This involves analysing aspects related to project management organisation and decision-making processes.
- **Innovation:** Evaluators seek out elements within the project that are innovative to the field of interest. This can include ideas, approaches or solutions that have been introduced which have not been tried before. Such innovation can enhance a project's impact, scalability and sustainability.
- **Impact:** Evaluators also focus on assessing the impact of the project. They examine both short- and long-term effects on the target group and stakeholders as well as a broader scale within their specific context. This includes considering any consequences of the project.
- **Sustainability:** When evaluating a project's sustainability, the evaluator carefully examines whether its benefits will continue after completion. This involves assessing factors such as the project's design, stakeholders' ability to maintain its outcomes and the availability of resources for support.
- **Scalability:** Evaluators assess whether the project's outcomes can be replicated or expanded to address issues in wider contexts or reach a wider audience. Therefore, it is crucial to plan for partnerships with countries or associations actively involved and networked widely in order to ensure long-term scalability, across Europe.
- **Engagement with target stakeholders:** Evaluators gauge how stakeholders have been connected to the project. They take into account the extent to which stakeholders have been consulted, involved and included in decision-making processes to ensure that their viewpoints and requirements have been properly taken care of.
- **Monitoring and evaluation (M&E):** Evaluators analyse the M&E system implemented by the project. This involves assess how well monitoring progress has been conducted in the measurement of outcomes using tools and indicators and how well the project reports articulate learning from implementation experiences.
- **Learning:** Evaluators consider the knowledge gained from the project, which can inform other projects and contribute to improving understanding in the field of interest. They analyse the achievements, challenges and failures identifying insights that can be applied to endeavours.

To summarise, the final evaluation is the ultimate authority in determining whether your project is viewed as successful by the funder. You therefore need to pay close attention to how you will report on your progress and how you prove that what you say you achieved is demonstrated. Overall project evaluations are indispensable for learning, growth and progress in this field. In the next chapter we review how you should articulate your final report.

## 8.5 The Final Report Delivery

As we indicated the final report is your chance to prove to the project evaluators that you have accomplished your project aims and objectives and delivered in terms of activities, results and dissemination. It is also an opportunity to highlight what you have done outside above and beyond what was expected.

The final report usually consists of three sections. These are the Narrative Report, the Timesheets and Publishing of outputs. Below we look at these sections in turn.

### *8.5.1 Narrative Report: The Process for Completing the Report*

You should set up a working group to write the narrative report. We recommend no more than three to four people in such a group, rather than the whole consortium partnership. As a rule this group should be composed of the Project Lead, the Quality Manager and one or two research assistants from within the project to support the narrative writing process.

You usually access the final report template through the relevant Agency portal. We recommend not writing the report directly into the portal but rather copying all relevant sections into a working draft document. This should then be discussed amongst the Working Group to identify the structure of the report and what you will need to do to complete it.

Once this discussion has taken place, the rest of the consortium partners should be contacted to supply data such as piloting results, workshop evaluations and dissemination activities.

Once a draft narrative is completed this should be circulated to all consortium partners for comment and edits. Following this activity you can then cut and paste the finalised draft into the relevant sections of the report template on the relevant Agency's port and submit.

Below we present and discuss as an example of this process how we completed the final report for the ERASMUS+ funded SSTeMM Report.

#### Background

The first section Background asked "Why did you apply for this project?" and "What were the need you have addressed?" We reviewed our original grant application and used this as inspiration for the first question. We referenced how we wanted to help nursing students develop personal resilience and empower them to manage stress and enhance their well-being. We also reiterated some of the negative impacts of work-related stress—the central problem we wanted to address—as well as some of the important guiding documents which laid the foundation for the project (for example, European Framework for Health and Well-being and the Who Framework of Action for Health Promoting Universities). We outlined the key resources we developed, the open-source nature of these resources and how this significantly supported European policy goals.

### Objectives

This section asked, "what did you want to achieve by implementing the project"? We reviewed the corresponding section of the original grant application and included a concise reiteration of these originally stated objectives. This included what we wanted to do, why we wanted to do it and how we wanted to do it.

### Implementation

This section asked, "what activities did you implement?". In this section, we outlined our main activities including the development of the mobile application, the learning management system and online materials, the four academic papers we wrote, the workshops and conferences we held.

### Results

This section asked, "What concrete outputs and other results did your project produce?". Here we named and described various outputs including our multilingual website; SSTeMM personal assessment tool, SSTeMM organisational assessment tool; SSTeMM mobile application; SSTeMM Moodle Platform; Cognitive Behavioural Therapy (CBT)-based resources, SSTeMM manual; academic papers.

### Description of the project

This section asked "please provide a summary of your project's concrete results and achievements. Were all original objectives of the project met? Please comment on any objectives initially pursued but not achieved and describe any achievements exceeding the initial expectations". In this section, we described our results and achievements highlighting, for example, data around the total number of downloads of the SSTeMM app, the number of people accessing the SSTeMM website and the number of survey respondents.

### *8.5.2 Financial Reporting*

- **Timesheets:** Properly prepared timesheets to the funder are important both for demonstrating the monitoring of resources used and reporting on the human resources employed in the conduct of project activities. Timesheets should be completed by all partners and checked frequently by the project lead. Activities should always be aligned to reports of activities. An overall total resource allocation for different categories (for example, "researcher" and "technical") per project partner was calculated and agreed clearly in writing (for example, per email). The timesheets and calculations were then handed to the Research Finance department which reviewed the submitted timesheets. Once figures were confirmed, the data were inputted into the project portal.
- **Workshops, meetings, project management and other expenses:** Workshops, meetings and other expenses are also cost categories that had to be recorded for each partner in the portal. The recording of workshops and meetings required information around where the workshop/meeting took place and the number of participants. Project management expenses were calculated automatically based on fixed rates. Other expenses had to be recorded where applicable.

### *8.5.3 Publishing and Other Outputs*

Project outputs were published on several platforms including the SSTeMM project website, social media, Open Science Framework and the EU's own portal. Outputs were published using Creative Commons Licences, where possible, in line with best practice.

## 8.6 Conclusion

To conclude, in this chapter we provided you with guidance on what evaluators look for in the report and principles for drafting the final report, drawing upon our record of success. The final report and demonstrating that you have achieved the key indicators as laid out in the original application is crucial for recognition by the EU or other funders that your project has been successful and well run. In the narrative within your report the key person to convince of your success is the evaluator who will assess your success against some key metrics. Providing a well-crafted, plain English report narrating your success with demonstrable evidence to support your claims is therefore crucial not only in terms of the outcome for your specific project but also in establishing your long-term credibility with funders, consortium partners and stakeholders for future funding applications.

**C.-Andreas Dalluege** Founder and Managing Partner of IBK Group; Chairman of the European Business Excellence Network e.V.; National Council Member of the Irish Work Study Institute. Certified Advisor & Trainer of EFQM, Operating Partner and Trainer of Initiative Ludwig-Erhard-Preis (ILEP). Since 1990 he participated as the senior researcher for his organisation in over 35 EU projects in most programme types offered by the EU and represented his company in all of them at the Management Board level as well as worked as our lead researcher in them.

He serves on the national board of the Irish Work Study Institute (IIESMS) and as President of the European Business Excellence Network (EuroBEN).

As a lecturer at the TH Aschaffenburg, he also gives classes on the design, proposing and running of EU Research projects since 2019. Contact: cad@ibk.eu

**Kasandra Musović** Ph.D. cand. and registered nurse, since 2019 academic nurse and researcher with primary research areas are in the science of caring and nursing education. She has worked on several projects: Student Stress Training e-Mobile Management (SSTeMM) and Erasmus Mundus Design Measures (EMDM): Design and Implementation of Master Degree in Palliative Care (DSGN-PALL-CARE); and is currently working on EU4Health project The Dynamic Digital skills for Medical and Allied Professions in Health Services (DDS-MAP). She is also a student member of the European Academy of Nursing Science and the International Association of Human Caring and International Exchange Alumni, Bureau of Educational and Cultural Affairs. Contact: kasandra.musovic1@um.si

**Florian Scheibein** is a Research Assistant and PhD student at the School of Health Sciences, South East Technological University. He is currently the Lead Research Assistant for an EU4Health project—DDS-MAP—and Grant Holder Manager for an EU COST Action—CUPID. He has been involved in three ERASMUS projects and was the co-recipient of the Council of Europe Pompidou Group European Drug Prevention Prize for one of these projects. He is an Editor for the Harm Reduction Journal and is a Co-Director and General Secretary of the Network of Early Career Professionals in Addiction Medicine which works with the World Health Organisation's Alcohol, Drugs and Addictive Behaviours Unit. Contact: Florian.Scheibein@setu.ie

**Gregor Štiglic** Professor and head of the Research Institute at the University of Maribor Faculty of Health Sciences. Since 2014, he has served as Vice Dean for Research at the same faculty, where he coordinates the research work of various research groups. He has led and worked on numerous research projects in digital healthcare and application of advanced artificial intelligence methods in healthcare.

In the past decade, he has served as a reviewer and panel member for different funding agencies such as EU Horizon Europe, UKRI Medical Research Council, The Netherlands Organisation for Scientific Research—NWO and The Research Council of Norway. Contact: gregor.stiglic@um.si

**John Stephen Gary Wells** PhD, FAAN, FNMFRCSI (Ad Eundem) is Dean of the School of Health Sciences at the South East Technological University. John graduated from the University of Manchester with a degree in history. Following graduation, he trained and practised as a mental health nurse in London, eventually managing one of the busiest acute psychiatric admission units in the capital. John then transitioned from a clinical practice role to an academic one in 1993, moving to Ireland in 1998 to take up an academic position there.

John is an active and experienced researcher. As either Principal Investigator or co-investigator he has won funding from national and EU-funded research programmes to the value of 12 million Euros. He is a member of the National Research Ethics Committee for Clinical Trials in Ireland and holds visiting professorships at UCD, Ireland, King's College London, UK and Maribor University, Slovenia. John has published 115 peer-reviewed papers, 7 technical reports (commissioned by regional, national and EU agencies), 9 book chapters and 1 book.

At the time of publication he is principal investigator for an EU4Health-funded project on enhancing the digital skills of the pan- European health care workforce. He is also chairperson of a COST Action on expanding the access of people with intellectual disabilities to cancer services.
Contact: john.wells@setu.ie

# Chapter 9
# Reflections on the SSTeMM Project Experience

**C.-Andreas Dalluege, Dominika Vrbnjak, Majda Pajnkihar, and John Stephen Gary Wells**

The SSTeMM project was a dynamic journey encompassing experiences that brought both difficulties and achievements along with valuable opportunities for learning. As we reflect upon this expedition, several important themes become apparent which, we think, are worth highlighting in this chapter.

## 9.1 Themes

### *9.1.1 That Emerged*

- **The Power of Collaboration**: The SSTeMM project truly emphasised the strength that collaboration can bring. Engaging with partners underscored the significance of communication, mutual respect and adaptability. Although navigating differing opinions and approaches posed challenges, at times it ultimately resulted in fulfilling outcomes.
- **Importance of Planning and Flexibility:** The project reinforced the importance of planning as mechanism through which to manage the unexpected. A

C.-A. Dalluege
IBK, Wiesbaden, Germany
e-mail: cad@ibk.eu

D. Vrbnjak · M. Pajnkihar
University Maribor, Maribor, Slovenia
e-mail: dominika.vrbnjak@um.si; majda.pajnkihar@um.si

J. S. G. Wells (✉)
South East Technological University, Waterford, Ireland
e-mail: john.wells@setu.ie



C.-A. Dalluege, J. S. G. Wells (eds.), *Navigating an EU Research Project*, Management for Professionals, https://doi.org/10.1007/978-3-031-70928-9_9

comprehensive project plan, consisting of goals, timelines and defined roles served as our guiding path at the beginning of the project. It also served to provide a template as to what we had to change to deal with the unforeseen circumstances that appeared because of the COVID 19 pandemic.

- The key thing here was thinking about how we could adapt the existing plan to the changed circumstances in which we found ourselves. Once we had reviewed the original plan against the challenges, we faced we were able to adjust it accordingly; striking balance between planning and flexibility. Without the original robust and detail project, we would have found it more difficult to reassess what we needed to change.
- **Overcoming challenges as mechanism for personal learning growth:** The journey of this project was characterised by hurdles. Some things were expected such as slippage in meeting pre-pandemic deadlines or balancing project tasks with extraneous commitments. However, these challenges paled into insignificance once the pandemic began. Overcoming these obstacles demanded resilience, creativity and determination. It was during these moments that we experienced some of our substantial growth and learning.
- **The Value of Communication:** The significance of communication emerged as a recurring theme. Regular meetings, clear documentation and open dialogue were essential for coordinating the project and maintaining relationships with partners. The transition to work due to the pandemic further emphasised the importance of communication tools and practices.
- **Personal Development:** SSTeMM served as a catalyst for professional and personal growth. Managing a project in the extraordinary context in which it took place pushed us to expand our capabilities to acquire skills and venture beyond our comfort zones. Junior researchers involved in the project particularly benefited from their development through this experience. The management of the project through the pandemic offered our junior researchers' opportunities for growth by developing as they took on more responsibility within the project as colleagues that were more senior were drawn into their institutional responsibilities. They thereby gained greater self-confidence and management experience than they otherwise would have had in normal circumstances.
- **The Joy of Accomplishment:** Finally, the feeling of fulfilment after completing the project through such a challenging time was profound. Witnessing and reporting the results of our work was incredibly satisfying.

To sum up the SSTeMM project has been an experience. The knowledge gained connections made and personal development achieved along this journey were priceless.

## 9.2 Doing Things More Effectively

Based on what we learned from the themes above below are some important areas to focus on for your future projects.

- **Early Catastrophic Risk Management Planning**: Although we did engage in planning taking more time for an in-depth initial planning phase could have helped us avoid difficulties later on. Bearing in mind the more uncertain world we now live in (climate change, war in Europe and possible future pandemics) we would now include a risk assessment to anticipate significant national and pan-European crises and how we would propose to mitigate their impact.
- **Improved Use of Technology**: Integrating collaboration tools right from the beginning would greatly facilitate seamless communication, especially in remote work situations. However, it is important to be cautious and anticipate any challenges associated with using technology in project management such as making things too complex or relying heavily on tools alone. To address these challenges effectively it is crucial that technology tools align with the project's requirements accompanied by sufficient training and support for users to use them effectively.
- **Streamlining timesheets:** Streamlining such processes as timesheets through automation or assigning roles to fill them in can help reduce stress and improve efficiency. To improve the management of timesheets it is essential to establish guidelines, provide training and utilise as simplified a format as is acceptable to the funder. Additionally regular reminders to partners as to the need to maintain efficient timesheet practices will save participants considerable stress as the project progresses.
- **More clearly define roles and associated functions:** To enhance the functioning of a project it is necessary to establish precise role definitions and clearly delineate tasks in order to avoid overlap of functions. One effective technique for defining project roles is using the RACI matrix. This technique categorises involvement in tasks as Responsible, Accountable, Consulted or Informed thereby establishing ownership and preventing any gaps or overlaps. By implementing this approach, we can streamline task execution. Improve decision-making clarity by ensuring allocation of responsibilities.
- **More effective internal communication:** To enhance project communication, it is important to set expectations for all team members while utilising an RACI matrix for role clarity. Additionally fostering a team culture that encourages dialogue plays a vital role in improving overall communication. Running meetings with defined agendas and encouraging questions for clarification are practices to consider. In some cases, investing in communication training may prove beneficial.
- **Being conscious of stressors on team members:** During the pandemic SSTeMM became a source of stress for all the members of the consortium partnerships involved. To improve projects, it would be advantageous to prioritise wellbeing among the team by implementing stress management strategies.

- The team can enhance their understanding of stress management techniques such as mindfulness, time management and relaxation exercises. This will help them develop coping mechanisms to address stress effectively. Taking care of oneself not only contributes to wellbeing but it also improves time management and enhances overall performance.
- Another source of stress is time management. Implementing time management strategies such as project management methodologies or software tools like time tracking apps, to-do list apps or calendar apps can help ensure a more balanced workload and reduce stress levels. However, it is crucial to avoid overcomplicating things with features when using tools. It is also important to provide training for user adoption and not overly rely on technology.
- **Learning and Adapting:** To prevent insights from being forgotten due to time gaps and team changes within a project initiate regular discussions, on lessons learned across the course of the project trajectory and keep a record of these. Reflection and review on lessons learned can facilitate the learning process for all members of the project team.

In conclusion, through thinking and thoughtful reflection, we can guide ourselves in projects to strive for improvement in project processes and outcomes.

## 9.3 Looking for New Opportunities

As we reflected on the SSTeMM project, we also looked forward to new opportunities. Below are some of our reflections on this.

- **Expanding the Scope:** The SSTeMM project focused primarily on nurse students. However, stress and mental health issues are pervasive in various population segments. Future projects, such as DDS-MAP (funded by EU4Health) and Work-Life-Flow (WLF, funded by ERASMUS+), therefore look to expand to other target groups, such as teachers, parents or employees in high-stress occupations and perhaps in everyday life.
- **Technology Integration:** The project underscored the potential of technology in managing stress and promoting mental wellbeing. This could be a focal point for future projects—developing innovative, tech-based interventions or leveraging existing technologies for the promotion of wellbeing. As technology continues to evolve, exploring the integration of virtual reality, apps and wearable devices could further enhance the effectiveness of stress management interventions.
- **Global Collaborations:** The SSTeMM project brought together partners from different countries, highlighting the value of diverse perspectives. To build upon this success, we seek additional international collaborations by actively networking at conferences, engaging through online platforms, leveraging existing contacts and tapping into a broader expertise and cultural insights. This not only enriches our work but also facilitates the cross-cultural validation and application

of our interventions, ensuring their relevance and effectiveness across diverse populations.

- **Policy Advocacy:** Presenting the results of the project to decision-makers can have a significant impact so that they incorporate the research evidence into recommendations to the wider population on the importance of promoting and protecting mental wellbeing.
- **Training and Capacity Building**: There is a clear need for building capacity in stress management. Future projects could focus on developing and delivering training programmes with tailored content for teachers, parents, managers and other key actors—we have created such content within DDS-MAP. This could create a ripple effect, empowering these individuals to promote mental health within their spheres of influence.
- **Partnerships with Industry**: Collaboration with industry can open new opportunities. For instance, technology companies can aid in stress management app development, while design and user experience firms contribute to user-friendly mental health apps. Partnerships with businesses extend mental health promotion to corporate environments, and collaborations with healthcare institutions ensure accuracy and data integration for enhanced effectiveness.
- **Sustainability:** Sustainability should be a key consideration in future projects. This includes ensuring the sustainability of the interventions developed and their long-term impact. For example, in relation to SSTeMM, mobile phones have become permanent personal "gadgets" for all generations. By promoting and updating mobile apps for stress management benefits, we can influence the impact of the benefits across a large and wide population.

## 9.4 Conclusion

In this chapter we have tried to convey the overall lessons that we learned during the SSTeMM project. Whilst SSTeMM proved at times to be highly stress inducing (which was ironic given its subject) for all members of the team, it also facilitated us to think differently about how to do things. One of the dangers of being successful in relation to grant winning and project implementation is that you can become too mechanistic in your approaches. The experience of working on SSTeMM provided us with an opportunity to refresh our thinking about project implementation and acquire or reconnect with a whole set of skills and approaches which in previous years of project management we had not used. SSTeMM therefore became for us an immensely valued experience of renewal.

**C.-Andreas Dalluege** Founder and Managing Partner of IBK Group; Chairman of the European Business Excellence Network e.V.; National Council Member of the Irish Work Study Institute. Certified Advisor & Trainer of EFQM, Operating Partner and Trainer of Initiative Ludwig-Erhard-Preis (ILEP).

Since 1990 he participated as the senior researcher for his organisation in over 35 EU projects in most programme types offered by the EU and represented his company in all of them at the Management Board level as well as worked as our lead researcher in them.

He serves on the national board of the Irish Work Study Institute (IIESMS) and as President of the European Business Excellence Network (EuroBEN).

As a lecturer at the TH Aschaffenburg, he also gives classes on the design, proposing and running of EU Research projects since 2019. Contact: cad@ibk.eu

**Dominika Vrbnjak** , Associate Professor at University of Maribor Faculty of Health Sciences is a member of Sigma Theta Tau International, Honour Society of Nursing, the European Academy of Nursing Science and the International Association of Human Caring. Her research interests include caring and safety and quality in nurse education and practice. She has experience with national and international projects related to pedagogical approaches in nursing and technology in nursing education. Contact: dominika.vrbnjak@um.si

**Majda Pajnkihar** Professor, PhD, RN, FAAN, FEANS, former Dean of the Faculty of Health Sciences, University of Maribor, Head of the Institute of Nursing care, Senior Researcher and Full Professor, who has been involved in numerous national and international projects. Her teaching experience includes work at numerous internationally renowned universities. She is a member of Sigma Theta Tau International, the Honour Society of Nurses and a Fellow of the American Academy of Nursing and the European Academy of Nursing Sciences. Contact: majda.pajnkihar@um.si

**John Stephen Gary Wells** PhD, FAAN, FNMFRCSI (Ad Eundem) is Dean of the School of Health Sciences at the South East Technological University. John graduated from the University of Manchester with a degree in history. Following graduation, he trained and practised as a mental health nurse in London, eventually managing one of the busiest acute psychiatric admission units in the capital. John then transitioned from a clinical practice role to an academic one in 1993, moving to Ireland in 1998 to take up an academic position there.

John is an active and experienced researcher. As either Principal Investigator or co-investigator he has won funding from national and EU-funded research programmes to the value of 12 million Euros. He is a member of the National Research Ethics Committee for Clinical Trials in Ireland and holds visiting professorships at UCD, Ireland, King's College London, UK and Maribor University, Slovenia. John has published 115 peer-reviewed papers, 7 technical reports (commissioned by regional, national and EU agencies), 9 book chapters and 1 book.

At the time of publication he is principal investigator for an EU4Health-funded project on enhancing the digital skills of the pan-European health care workforce. He is also chairperson of a COST Action on expanding the access of people with intellectual disabilities to cancer services. Contact: john.wells@setu.ie

# Chapter 10
# Concluding Messages

**C.-Andreas Dalluege and John Stephen Gary Wells**

We stated at the beginning of this book that our aim was to provide you, the reader, tools, knowledge and confidence to make a successful submission for EU funding to support your project and our experience of how to manage a project successfully. We want this book to be supportive of your endeavours by sharing our project management experience gained over thirty years and referencing a recent project, SSTeMM, to provide you with a 'real-world' example of project management.

In this, the final, chapter we highlight the key messages we think are important for you to take away from this book. In addition, we make some suggestions that we think the EU should consider to improve the applicants' experience of the project application process and support the project implementation process.

## 10.1 Some Key Messages to Remember for a Successful Project Outcome

Our experience indicates that the potential success for a proposal is reliant on a well-prepared and clearly explained narrative that is succinct and precise. Remember that English (the official language for a submission) for many evaluators is their second language so choose simple plain language instead of overly complex and technical language.

---

C.-A. Dalluege (✉)
IBK, Wiesbaden, Germany
e-mail: cad@ibk.eu

J. S. G. Wells
South East Technological University, Waterford, Ireland
e-mail: john.wells@setu.ie



C.-A. Dalluege, J. S. G. Wells (eds.), *Navigating an EU Research Project*, Management for Professionals, https://doi.org/10.1007/978-3-031-70928-9_10

The narrative should emphasise that ALL partners within a consortium are credible and capable of delivering their input based on their previous record in the field of interest. Your consortium should also demonstrate a breadth of membership from across the EU regions.

A proposal needs to be clearly targeted in terms of the problem it addresses and the stakeholders it will involve. Above all, a proposal needs to explain how it supports EU policy in the chosen area of interest. That, combined with a logical work plan coupled with a transparent budget is key to making a convincing case that your project is worth funding.

Running the project requires planning and managing budgets to ensure long-term financial sustainability, regularly reporting on performance, addressing risks as they arise. This starts with preparing a document with all relevant cooperation, communication and risk management rules to be discussed and formally agreed on during the project's 'kick-off' meeting. Deciding early on how future amendments in relation to unforeseen circumstances will be managed and implemented will help substantially to reduce individual stress and ensure that the project does not get side tracked or paralysed by such circumstances.

Do not forget to allocate sufficient resource and time for seeking ethical approval (if necessary) and testing and localisation of any instruments and/or product, for example surveys or teaching modules. Many project teams forget that all relevant results must be available on all project partner languages and then get stressed at the project end phase when they suddenly remember this fact and rapidly must translate outputs into local languages.

The final report and demonstrating that you have achieved the key indicators as laid out in the original application is crucial for recognition by the EU or other funders that your project has been successful and well run. The final report is normally required to be delivered post the funding period (usually for EU-funded projects this is two months after the formal end date of the project).

Preparing and finalising the report demands a high degree of effort on the part of the co-ordinator and partners. Remember such demanding activity and input is unfunded so make sure your partners start to prepare this work during the run-up to the formal end project end date when resources can still be costed to the budget.

In the narrative within your report the key person to convince of your success is the evaluator. The evaluator will assess your success against some key metrics. Providing a well-crafted, plain English report narrating your success with demonstrable evidence to support your claims is therefore crucial not only in terms of the outcome for your specific project but also in establishing your long-term credibility with funders, consortium partners and stakeholders for future funding applications.

The key message to take away from the above and the content of this book is that above all you need to be conscious that your consortium's endeavours remain feasible, cost-effective and impactful within the funded timelines and sustainable beyond the funded timeline; and that you communicate this clearly to all stakeholders, including your final evaluator.

## 10.2 Improving the Support of Applicants When Making a Submission

Bearing in mind that many of our EU projects deal with stress in the workplace, it would be surprising if we are not aware of how stress inducing a project application can be, particularly in relation to meeting a submission deadline. It is our experience that no matter how expert one is in making project applications, the process remains for all involved a stressful one.

Of course, a certain degree of stress in life is unavoidable. Indeed, a limited amount of stress can enhance an individual's performance (Jessop, 2019). However, there is also a tipping point where stress can become destructive in terms of both performance and personal health impacts. Undue external pressures and system frustrations beyond the control of an individual often cause this type of stress (Barbayannis et al., 2022).

The European Pact for Mental Health and Well-being (2008) called for an improvement in the health, quality of life and resilience of EU citizens and recognised workplace settings as a source of mental ill health. EU rhetoric has emphasised that member states need to take action to promote mental health and well-being in the workplace. However, the European Commission has been criticised for not taking concrete steps in relation to legislation, particularly as this relates to stress in the workplace (Yarmolyuk-Kröck, 2022; Ståhl, 2023). The EC framework directive on health and safety (89/391/EEC) places a duty on employers 'to ensure the safety and health of workers in every aspect related to their work'.

Whilst there is an absence of legislation underpinning these calls, this does not preclude the European Commission from operationalising mental health and well-being rhetoric into its practices and operations. One area we suggest is the funding application process in relation to research calls. As noted in Chap. 3, the EU submission portals can often be a cause of stress for researchers making an application.

The funding portal is often complicated to navigate and its lack of an intuitive design means that many hours can be wasted either by not entering data in the right place or missing areas in which you have to enter data (as we indicated in Chap. 3). Whilst as a rule generally the portal will alert you to areas where you are required to enter data, this is not always immediately apparent.

As you may recall we described one experience where we had to re-enter a considerable amount of financial detail (much of it already submitted in a different section of the application) into an addendum to the application of which we only became aware the night before the closing date for the submission. The applicant team were up throughout the night entering the data, which ran to close to 300 extra pages to the application. This resulted in one of the teams getting a stress-related illness that took him a week from which to recover.

Exacerbating these issues is that there is no uniform portal design and submission form for all programmes. Despite recent changes, which have established single portal access point for most programmes, the portal and submission still can vary from one funding programme to another. This means an applicant must navigate a completely new portal/form in making a submission. This familiarisation process can take a considerable amount of time. Submission portals are also subject to change from year-to-year, sometimes subtly other times more significant changes are made. Either way such changes can often add to the burden of submission.

We have also experienced portal crashes (which is one of the reasons why we recommend working on your application in MS-Word rather than directly in the portal as a crash can lead to you losing your work). Whilst overall the technical support alerts applicants quickly when this happens, it is nevertheless stress inducing, particularly when a resolution of the issue can, on occasion, take some time. Sometimes the EU extends the deadline for submission because of such issues, but this is not always the case.

Having highlighted the issues in the application process that can cause stress, what do we recommend for the EU to consider? Firstly, we would recommend producing both a portal and application form that is uniform across all funding programmes. This would greatly alleviate applicant stress. Secondly, ensure that the guidance highlights in clear plain English all the sections that need to be addressed. Thirdly, highlight any changes to the portal from the previous year on the platform. The National Contact Points' briefings in relation to a specific call often highlights such changes; but this assumes that all interested parties can access these. This is not always the case so having specific written explanation of changes on the platform itself would be highly beneficial. Finally, we would suggest that the EU make explicit to applicants a policy/criterion about submission date timeline extensions as this relates to the number and length of portal crashes. This would establish a uniform approach across programmes and remove uncertainty for applicants.

## 10.3 Reflections on Writing This Book and Conclusion

We, the authors, have gained considerably from writing this book. The writing process is the first opportunity we have had as researchers to look back and reflect on our achievements, what we got right and what we could improve upon. It has enabled us also to tabulate and narrate our processes for making an application and managing our projects. This is something that we have rather taken for granted in terms of our accumulated experience but never written down.

In relation to the unprecedented events surrounding the COVID pandemic and accompanying global 'lockdown', this book has facilitated a certain degree of catharsis and reminiscence—it was quite easy to forget the degree of stress we all came under and felt during this time. Reflecting back has also highlighted for us the pivotal role the National Agency and National Contact Point played in helping to alleviate our stress at this time in relation to the SSTeMM project. We are and remain very grateful to the support they gave. In turn, it highlights the key role and duty of the National Contact Point, National Agency and EU in making researchers feel supported, even when there is not a global emergency.

Finally, we hope you have found reading this book a useful contribution to your thinking about how you will write an application and the things you need to consider in both the application for funding and the management of a project. We also hope, to some degree, you have found the book reassuring as we highlight that making an application for funding and management of a funded project is challenging regardless of the experience of the applicant. We remain, like you, on a learning curve!

**C.-Andreas Dalluege** Founder and Managing Partner of IBK Group; Chairman of the European Business Excellence Network e.V.; National Council Member of the Irish Work Study Institute. Certified Advisor & Trainer of EFQM, Operating Partner and Trainer of Initiative Ludwig-Erhard-Preis (ILEP).

Since 1990 he participated as the senior researcher for his organisation in over 35 EU projects in most programme types offered by the EU and represented his company in all of them at the Management Board level as well as worked as our lead researcher in them.

He serves on the national board of the Irish Work Study Institute (IIESMS) and as President of the European Business Excellence Network (EuroBEN).

As a lecturer at the TH Aschaffenburg, he also gives classes on the design, proposing and running of EU Research projects since 2019. Contact: cad@ibk.eu

**John Stephen Gary Wells** PhD, FAAN, FNMFRCSI (Ad Eundem) is Dean of the School of Health Sciences at the South East Technological University. John graduated from the University of Manchester with a degree in history. Following graduation, he trained and practised as a mental health nurse in London, eventually managing one of the busiest acute psychiatric admission units in the capital. John then transitioned from a clinical practice role to an academic one in 1993, moving to Ireland in 1998 to take up an academic position there.

John is an active and experienced researcher. As either Principal Investigator or co-investigator he has won funding from national and EU-funded research programmes to the value of 12 million Euros. He is a member of the National Research Ethics Committee for Clinical Trials in Ireland and holds visiting professorships at UCD, Ireland, King's College London, UK and Maribor University, Slovenia. John has published 115 peer-reviewed papers, 7 technical reports (commissioned by regional, national and EU agencies), 9 book chapters and 1 book.

At the time of publication he is principal investigator for an EU4Health-funded project on enhancing the digital skills of the pan-European health care workforce. He is also chairperson of a COST Action on expanding the access of people with intellectual disabilities to cancer services. Contact: john.wells@setu.ie

# Appendix A: European Research Funding

The EU runs a wide range of research-oriented programmes that offer a range of projects. To do so, a vast budget is reserved. As an example, already the HORIZON programme has an allocated budget of 95,500 Million EUR for the years 2021–2027. To keep control of such big sums, the EU applies strict rules, for tight control over how funds are used and to ensure money is spent in a transparent, accountable manner.

EU funding comes in many different forms:

- grants—typically, people apply for grants by submitting ideas for projects following a "call for proposals"
- subsidies managed by national or regional authorities
- loans, guarantees and equity as forms of financial assistance to support EU policies and programmes
- loans to EU Member States and non-EU countries
- prizes for winners of Horizon Europe contests.

Programmes funded by the EU budget can be managed in three different ways:

- **direct management**: EU funding is managed directly by the European Commission. You can apply for this type of funding by answering calls for proposals managed directly by the EU.
- **shared management**: Shared management of EU funding means that responsibility for running a given programme is shared jointly between the European Commission and national authorities in EU countries. Around 70% of EU programmes are run this way. The EU "opens" in such cases the call for proposals, but whilst the whole call as a common red line, the specific aims and objectives may differ a bit from country to country.
- **indirect management**: Indirect management of EU funding means that the funding programmes are partly or fully implemented by third parties, such as



C.-A. Dalluege, J. S. G. Wells (eds.), *Navigating an EU Research Project*, Management for Professionals, https://doi.org/10.1007/978-3-031-70928-9

national authorities or international organisations. Funding takes the form of subsidies, which you apply for at national level.

The research topics are managed under 6 headings each of which represents several programmes

## Heading 1: Single Market, Innovation and Digital

### *Research & Innovation*

**Horizon Europe**: Scientific, technological, economic, environmental and societal impact; support to all forms of research and innovation.

**Euratom Research and Training Programme**: Euratom aims to pursue nuclear research and training activities with an emphasis on continually improving nuclear safety, security and radiation protection.

**ITER**: Ambitious international project to build the world's biggest fusion machine, advance fusion energy technology for a greener and more sustainable energy mix.

European Strategic Investments

**InvestEU:** Providing the EU with crucial long-term funding, crowding in private investment, supporting the recovery and a greener, more digital and resilient Europe.

**Connecting Europe Facility:** Supporting the delivery of key energy, transport and digital infrastructure across Europe.

**Digital Europe Programme:** The Digital Europe Programme is the first EU programme that aims to accelerate the recovery and drive the digital transformation of Europe.

Single Market

**Single Market Programme:** Empowering and protecting consumers; ensuring food safety, enabling EU small- and medium-sized enterprises to thrive.

**EU Anti-Fraud Programme:** Protection of the EU's financial interests; specialised equipment, knowledge and training.

**Cooperation in the field of taxation (FISCALIS):** The Fiscalis programme enables national tax administrations to create and exchange information and expertise.

**Cooperation in the field of customs (CUSTOMS):** Customs supports the cooperation between customs authorities and protects the financial and economic interests of the EU and its Member States.

**Space**

**European Space Programme:** EU space policy; satellite technology and innovation; data, navigation and communication services; fighting climate change; disaster response.

## Heading 2: Cohesion and Values

### *Regional Development & Cohesion*

**European Regional Development Fund (ERDF):** Strengthening EU economic, social and territorial cohesion by correcting imbalances between regions through programmes implemented by local authorities.

**Cohesion Fund (CF):** The Cohesion Fund aims to reduce economic and social disparities and to promote sustainable development.

**REACT-EU**: Additional funding for the existing 2014–2020 cohesion programmes under ERDF, ESF and FEAD.

**Support to the Turkish Cypriot community**: The Aid Programme aims to facilitate the reunification of Cyprus.

Recovery and Resilience

**Recovery and Resilience Facility**: The Recovery and Resilience Facility is the key instrument of NextGenerationEU to help the EU emerge stronger and more resilient from the current crisis.

**Technical Support Instrument**: The Technical Support Instrument provides tailor-made technical expertise to EU countries to carry out reforms.

**Protection of the Euro Against Counterfeiting**: Prevent and combat counterfeiting and related fraud and preserve the integrity of the euro banknotes and coins.

**Union Civil Protection Mechanism (rescEU)**: Strengthen cooperation between the EU Member States and 6 Participating States in the field of civil protection.

**EU4Health**: Investing in resilient, equitable and modern health systems, improving the health of EU citizens and protecting people from cross-border health threats.

**Investing in People, Social Cohesion & Values**

**European Social Fund+**: The European Social Fund+ (ESF+) is the EU's main instrument for investing in people with the aim of building a more social and inclusive Europe.

**Erasmus+:** Support the educational, professional and personal development of people in education, training, youth and sport.

**European Solidarity Corps:** For young people wishing to volunteer to help the disadvantaged, provide humanitarian aid, contribute to health and environmental action.

**Justice Programme:** Strengthening democracy, rule of law and fundamental rights.

**Citizens, Equality, Rights and Values Programme:** Protection and promotion of the rights and values as enshrined in the EU Treaties and the Charter of Fundamental Rights.

**Creative Europe:** Creative Europe is the European Commission's programme for providing support to the culture and audiovisual sectors.

## Heading 3: Natural Resources & Environment

### *Agriculture & Maritime Policy*

**European Agricultural Guarantee Fund (EAGF):** The EAGF funds income support for EU farmers and measures to stabilise agricultural markets.

**European Agricultural Fund for Rural Development (EAFRD):** The EAFRD provides funding to support rural areas and strengthen the EU's agri-food and forestry sectors.

**European Maritime, Fisheries and Aquaculture Fund:** Common fisheries policy, maritime policy, aquaculture, sustainable development.

Environment & Climate Action

**Programme for the Environment and Climate Action (LIFE):** To achieve the shift towards a sustainable, circular and resilient economy, protect and restore the environment, halt and reverse biodiversity loss.

**Just Transition Fund:** Supporting the transition towards climate neutrality by alleviating its socio-economic impact in the regions most affected.

## Heading 4: Migration & Border Management

### *Migration*

**Asylum, Migration and Integration Fund:** Migration, Asylum and Integration; Common European Asylum System; Migration Management; Solidarity.

### Border Management

**Integrated Border Management Fund:** Border Management; EU Common Visa Policy; European Border and Coast Guard, Custom Control Equipment at Customs Border points and Customs laboratories.

## Heading 5: Security & Defence

### *Security*

**Internal Security Fund:** Security of the Union; Tackling radicalisation, terrorism, cybercrime, organised crime; Protecting victims of crime.

**Nuclear Decommissioning (Lithuania):** Ensuring safe closure of old nuclear reactors, protecting the environment and human health.

**Nuclear Safety and Decommissioning:** Ensuring safe closure of old nuclear reactors, protecting the environment and human health.

### Defence

**European Defence Fund:** The European Defence Fund is the Commission's key initiative to support, with the EU budget, collaborative research and development of defence capabilities.

## Heading 6: Neighbourhood & the World

### *External Action*

**Global Europe: Neighbourhood, Development and International Cooperation Instrument:** Global Europe is the EU's main financial tool to contribute to sustainable development, peace and stability across the globe.

**Humanitarian Aid:** Whenever there is a disaster or humanitarian emergency, the EU provides assistance for the affected countries and populations.

**Common Foreign and Security Policy:** The CFSP contributes to the objectives of preserving peace, preventing conflicts and strengthening international security.

**Overseas Countries and Territories:** Promoting economic and social development of the Overseas Countries and Territories, increasing their resilience and competitiveness, reducing vulnerability.

# Appendix B: Some EU Projects Which We Have Either Led or Partnered

Collectively, we have been involved in approximately 60 EU-funded projects since 1990. To give you a better understanding of the range/scope of projects and their results as expected by the funding agencies of the EU, in Appendix B we give you short summaries of nine projects which we have either led or participated in as consortium partners. Some of these projects, for example DDS-MAP, have been quoted in the narrative of this book as exemplars to illustrate general points.

## BITTMAS: Business Transformation Towards Digitisation and Smart Systems

**Funding Agency:** ERASMUS+, BiBB (National Agency Germany)

**Active project years:** 2016–2019

**Active link:** https://www.esb-business-school.de/en/research/research-activities/bittmas

**Membership of Consortium by country**: Austria, Germany, (Co-ordinator), Ireland, Romania, Spain, Turkey

**Aim:** The project Business Transformation towards Digitisation and Smart Systems (BITTMAS) was launched to support small- and medium-sized enterprises (SMEs) in the digitisation and implementation of smart systems. The aim of BITTMAS was:

- to develop ways to efficiently provide information, new methods and solutions
- to gather knowledge and experience centrally to enable companies to access new technologies, processes and structures
- to support companies in evaluating new tools with regard to their potential for improvement and to be able to revise their company models if necessary



C.-A. Dalluege, J. S. G. Wells (eds.), *Navigating an EU Research Project*, Management for Professionals, https://doi.org/10.1007/978-3-031-70928-9

**Objectives:** The main objective of BITTMAS was to develop a user-oriented approach for trainers, staff and managers of SMEs. This was driven through web-based training modules, a self-assessment tool for potential analysis, the creation of a roadmap and a catalogue of measures, as well as autonomous planning and implementation of improvements.

**Results:** The BITTMAS Release Candidate, consisted of a web-based open-source library, the self-assessment tool for potential analysis and training as well as coaching modules, expands the range of high-quality learning opportunities for adults and strengthens the core competencies in training curricula.

## DELAROSE: Delivering E-Learning Accreditation to Reduce Occupational Stress in Employment

**Funding Agency**: Leargas (Irish National Agency as part of the Education, Audiovisual and Culture Executive Agency, European Union)

**Active project years**: 2013–2015

**Active link**: No longer active

**Membership of Consortium by country:** Ireland (co-ordinator) Austria, Belgium, Switzerland, United Kingdom

**Aim**: Drawing upon the results of the previously funded ROSE project to develop an accredited online learning pan-European programme for health and social care workers to manage their work-related stress.

**Objectives:**

Make a unique and significant contribution to the field of pan-European accreditation by developing and accrediting a course within the European Credit Transfer System (ECTS) for health and social care workers

Cross reference ECTS course to an equivalency within the European Credit system for Vocational Education and Training (ECVET) framework.

Pilot a system of common credit recognition between higher and vocational education in Europe to promote learner mobility

Map system indicators to higher education learning outcomes, so that a learner who achieves the learning requirements, can be accredited for that learning.

**Results:**

A fully ECTS accredited Level 6 online course with equivalency under ECVET for health and social care workers to manage their work-related stress provided by three of the higher education institutions.

This course continues to be provided by one of the partners (in a more developed format and at Level 8 ECTS). This course may be found at https://www.setu.ie/courses/certificate-in-management-of-occupational-stress-and-well-being.

## DSGN-PALL-CARE: Design and Implementation of Master Degree in Palliative Care

**Funding Agency:** European Union, Erasmus Mundus Design Measures

**Active project years:** 2022–2023

**Active link:** https://www.fzv.um.si/sites/default/files/projekti/EN%20Design%20and%20implementation%20of%20master%20degree%20in%20Palliative%20care%20programme_0.pdf

**Membership of Consortium by country:** Croatia (co-ordinator), Slovenia, Bosnia and Herzegovina

**Aim**: The DSGN-PALL-CARE) is an Erasmus Mundus project and was aimed at designing and developing a fully integrated and sustainable joint Master study programme in palliative care proposal providing state-of-the-art transnational education and training practices in palliative care, answering the growing need for palliative care providers and raising the awareness on the importance and necessity of palliative care among the general public in the EU and broader.

**Objectives**: Given the rising need for palliative care services, there is also a growing need for highly educated professionals who will provide those services. As Master level university education in palliative care is available in a few countries, the project explored the best practices and innovations abroad and encouraged students to seize the mobility opportunities.

**Results**: Identification of the need to improve the knowledge and competencies of teaching staff for the development, implementation and continuous improvement of learning by working to acquire the necessary competencies during the 15 months of project implementation and allowed their further development after the project end. The partners exchanged knowledge and best practices through regular communication, meetings and a study visit.

## DDS-MAP: Dynamic Digital Skills for Medical and Allied Professions

**Funding Agency:** EU4Health

**Active project years**: 2023–2025

**Website Active link:** https://ddsmap.easpd.eu/

**Membership of Consortium by country:** Ireland (co-ordinator), Belgium, Croatia, Germany, Italy, Latvia, Lithuania, Poland, Slovenia, Spain

**Aim:** The EU4Health-funded "DDS-MAP" project aims to develop new training provision for qualified EU healthcare and allied professionals focused on the acquisition and mastery of new digital technologies in the delivery of care services. Healthcare professionals' awareness, knowledge and self-reflection on their use of digital technologies will be explored through learning activities and professional practice.

**Objectives:**

- Map the provision of the digital skills (literacy, digital transformation, cybersecurity, online communication) of the health workforce at regional and European level
- Enable healthcare managers to better respond to current and emerging healthcare issues (cybersecurity, surge management, supply management).
- Enable healthcare workers to effectively plan, deliver, monitor and evaluate digital health care approaches and their well-being and resilience through adaptation of digital skills.
- Engage with regulatory authorities and professional associations to promote micro learning and credentials accreditation for the acquisition and recognition of digital skills.

**Results:**
We expect to generate the following results:

- A first-of-its-kind survey of the digital competences of the health care workforce across the European Union.
- European training modules developed through a co-creation process, addressing the needs of multiple disciplines such as hospital doctors, nurses and non-clinical staff.
- Micro credentials that leverage an established framework for DDS-MAP.
- Augmented and virtual reality (AR and VR) platform leveraging expertise within DDS-MAP to deliver educational content and skills assessment as part of a suite innovative work-based training.

## EDU-MENT: Education in Mental Health for Nurses in Home and Residential Care

**Funding Agency:** Erasmus+ Vocational Education and Training Form ID. KA220-VET-2FD42AAD

**Active project years:** 2024–2026

**Active link**: https://edu-ment.eu/

**Membership of Consortium by country:** Austria (co-ordinator), Slovenia, Cyprus

**Aim**: High-quality and web-based materials from international experts in teaching, research and practice for effective vocational training and higher education will be made available for other interested educational institutions. Together with the instructional design framework that we will develop as part of the project, this will enable vocational and higher education institutions to develop their own certificate courses more efficiently for specialised continuing education.

**Objectives**: The ensure of a blended learning training of 5 ECTS credit points aims to enhance the digital and professional competence of RNs in home-care and residential care facilities in the early detection, control and combat to mental health issues among clients in need of care as well as to strengthen their institutional implementation. This will enable RNs to better reach these clients and provide them with targeted support in accessing informal and formal service providers.

**Results**: The project will develop certified education for RNs as well as a methodology to address the three main challenges in the early detection, monitoring and response to mental health issues in home-care and residential care:

- understanding and standardised care
- interprofessional qualification of RNs
- operational and organisational qualification.

## ExCurS: An Excellence-Based Curriculum for the Improvement of LEAN & GREEN Management Skills in SME

**Funding Agency:** ERASMUS+, National Agency Spain

**Active project years**: 2022–2025

**Active link:** https://www.excurs.eu/

**Membership of Consortium by country:** Croatia, Germany, Ireland, Romania and Spain (co-ordinator)

**Aim**: An Excellence-based self-assessment tool that allows an organisation to easily identify improvement potentials as a basis for redesigning processes; suitable for digitalisation and revitalising existing business models by specific trainings; especially increase the competencies of managers and staff as well as the maturity of the SME towards digitalisation and sustainable organisation.

The overall goal of this project is to create a training programme for vocational education. ExCurS aims to offer a self-assessment tool that allows a match of organisational needs for skills and knowledge for a strategic growth with the personal development plan of individuals based on assessing existing and future potentials.

**Objectives**: To develop an overview of existing management and process management tools that support LEAN, Green and Digital Transformation requirements with a company specific recommendation list of tools and methods to learn about identified via a web-based self-assessment tool. The solution will be validated by delivering and piloting a training programme focussed on teaching LEAN & Green Management Skills for SME, thus supporting the EU new Green deal and by its hybrid training structure the digitalisation efforts.

**Results**: We expect to generate the following results:

- Up to 90 management methods and tools identified and listed.
- Web-based introduction tutorials for around 45 that are closest related to LEAN, Green and Digital Transformation management issues In English)

- Localisation of the 10 tutorials most relevant for all levels of staff to all consortium languages
- An Excellence-related self-assessment that identifies the most relevant company-specific topics and helps to identify potential knowledge gaps in dealing with the upcoming developments

## IMPRESS: Improving Management Competences on Excellence-Based Stress Avoidance and Working Towards Sustainable Organisational Development in Europe

**Funding Agency:** ERASMUS+ Innovation Alliance, Programme Office Brussels

**Active project years:** 2017–2020

**Active link:** https://www.excellence-in-stress-management.eu/

**Membership of Consortium by country**: Germany, Ireland, Latvia, Spain (Co-ordinator)

**Aim**: IMPRESS aims at developing insight on "work-related stress" issues in health and social care organisation, with the goal to develop approaches for early recognition of stress potentials and training modules that allow reacting to them and preventing the outbreak of stress.

**Objectives**:

The consortium analysed the impact of all aspects of the business including personnel, management style, work organisation and organisational structure, work–life balance, demographic changes and the need of upgrading unskilled and skilled workers, information overflow through modern communication expectations, stress caused by poor fit with the workplace (e.g. when people accept jobs below their skill levels in order to avoid unemployment), physical and mental health issues (e.g. linked to ergonomic issues, working hours and routines).

Besides work-based learning for people already employed in the organisations, the project also focused on how young people must be prepared in order to sustain their health and their employment until retirement in an economic situation where changing employers and sectors is becoming part of a regular employment history.

**Results**:

- An education module based on experiences in industry which equips professionals with the necessary knowledge and skill sets needed to deal with the work-related stress issues that occur in a continuously changing work environment.
- A "suite of practical tools" that can be used by suitably trained professionals to quantify stress levels in an organisation and at an individual level, especially with regard to the ability to work under pressure.
- An appropriate training approach for young people with the objective to enable them to cope with the challenges on the labour market by reducing the stress factors either before being employed or when they start their professional career.

- An individual self-assessment tool that allows a self-assessment to identify personal stress factors and potential resources.
- An organisational self-assessment tool that allows to anonymously accumulate the individual stress potentials to identify common factors for which the organisation then can offer interventions
- A book on all project results published by Springer (Berger, R., Dalluege, C.-A, Franz, HW; Organisational Excellence and Resilience: Stress Management as a Component of a Sustainable Corporate Development Strategy, Springer Nature Switzerland AG, 2022)

## ROSE: Reducing Occupational Stress in Employment

**Funding Agency:** Education, Audiovisual and Culture Executive Agency, European Union

**Active project years:** 2010 and 2012

**Active link**: No longer active

**Membership of Consortium by country:** Ireland (co-ordinator), Austria, Belgium, Italy, Romania, United Kingdom.

**Aim:** To help reduce stress and burnout amongst people working in the mental health and intellectual disability occupational support sector.

**Objectives:**

- Develop a combined person and work-directed stress management programme to improve the long-term retention within services of staff in this area.
- Provide an accessible and user-friendly online stress management programme which will be freely available to services and individuals 24 hours a day.

**Results:**

- Survey data on stress levels of the population of interest in five EU countries
- A short online open access self-help programme focused on social inclusion, workplace support, policy harmonisation and mental health
- Provision of data and a platform for the development of a further funding proposal entitled DELAROSE.

## SAETO Projects: Self-Assessment for Educational and Training Organisation

**Funding Agency:** Leonardo da Vinci Programme, div. National Agencies

**Active project years:** 2005–2015

**Active link:** http://www.saeto.eu/en/index.htm

The SAETO project family was a series of **seven interlinked research projects** of the EU's Leonardo da Vinci Programme, running between 2005 and 1015.

**Membership of Consortia by country:** Lichtenstein (co-ordinator for the initial submission to set up the SAETO series—further projects were then co-ordinated by other partners in the list of participating countries), Austria, Belgium, Czech Republic, Denmark, Germany, Ireland, Italy, Latvia, Netherlands, Portugal, Slovakia, Slovenia, Spain, Switzerland, Turkey, United Kingdom

**Aims:** SAETO (Self-Assessment for Educational and Training Organisation) dealt with the adaptation of the European Excellence Models (CAF, EFQM, Project Excellence) to the language and reality of Education and Training Organisations and with the dissemination and validation of the results in different countries.

Based on the original SAETO Project (2005–2007) two spin-off projects (TI-SAETO & Trans-SAETO, 2008–2010) extended, improved and fine-tuned the tools and training materials taking into account the participants' language and cultural background and being validated with over 85 pilots, thus developing a European Standard that respects local requirements.

End of 2011 the SAETO project family was enlarged by the Leonardo da Vinci Projects ACES, Design for Excellence and EVET that extended the number of reported case studies by another 30 pilots.

In mid-2013, representatives of all 6 SAETO projects joined in the LdV Partnership Project "SAETO-Web" to develop a common platform for marketing and supporting the SAETO Solution.

**Results**: The results were a continually growing toolset for self-assessment within educational and training organisations. The underlying approach was published as a book called IQM (Integrated Quality Management) that saw 4 reprintings with new results and a complete set of new case studies for each edition, covering a total of over 130 pilot cases.

## SSTeMM: Student Stress Training e-Mobile Management

**Funding Agency:** ERASMUS+, Higher Education Authority, National Agency Ireland.

Active project years: 2019–2022

**Website Active link**: https://sstemm.eu/

**Membership of Consortium by country:** Ireland (co-ordinator), Germany, Slovenia, Spain

**Aim:** To develop an end-user (which we define as internship student, internship mentor, hosting industry and HEI staff) accessible digital mobile platform of targeted work-based education, competency training and in vivo self-reflection learning opportunities to equip students and mentoring workers with the knowledge, skills and competencies to address occupational stressors (both personal and environmental).

**Objectives:**

- Develop and implement a stress self-assessment tool for staff and student nurses
- Develop and trial a mobile application that supports the development of personal skills to build student nurse resilience whilst on clinical placement
- Develop educational support materials for clinical mentors to use to support students in relation to student nurse stress
- Equip such students with reinforced skills and competency set that will enhance their personal well-being once they have entered the world of full-time employment following graduation/qualification.

**Results:**
All results can be found at https://sstemm.eu/

- A stress self-assessment tool
- A downloadable mobile application to help students manage their stress whilst on clinical placement
- A manual for staff to use to support students to manage their stress
- Resources relating to COVID-19 and lockdown

## Train4Health: Improving Healthcare Students' Competences for Behaviour Change to Effectively Support Self-Care in Chronic Diseases

**Funding Agency:** Education, Audiovisual and Culture Executive Agency, European Union

**Active project years:** 2019–2022

**Active link**: https://www.train4health.eu

**Membership of Consortium by country:** Portugal (co-ordinator), Ireland, Slovenia, Netherlands, Belgium, Portugal, Portugal

**Aim**: To address the unsatisfactory adherence to medication and lifestyle changes in chronic diseases, which led to health complications and increased costs, threatening the sustainability of healthcare systems.

**Objectives**: To improve health care students' competences for behaviour change; to effectively support self-care in chronic disease through an innovative educational package.

**Results**: The outcomes included improved competencies for students in supporting self-care in chronic diseases, overcoming gaps in behaviour change support education, and potentially enhancing employability and mobility for health professionals. For higher education institutions, the project aimed to increase transnational cooperation, improve curricula and training quality and offer flexible digital learning resources. Ultimately, Train4Health aimed to have a positive societal impact by improving self-care and lifestyle for people with chronic diseases, alleviating the individual and societal burden of these conditions.

## TRANSiTON: Digital TRANSition and dIgiTal resIlience in ONcology

**Funding Agency:** EU4Health

**Active project years:** 2023–2025

**Active link:** https://www.europeancancer.org/eu-projects/resource/transition

**Membership of Consortium by country:** Cyprus (co-ordinator), Belgium, Spain, Croatia, Germany, Portugal, Greece, Lithuania, Poland, Romania, Italy, France, Hungary, Bulgaria, Slovenia

**Aim**: The TRANSiTION project is developing an advanced education programme for healthcare professionals and non-clinical staff (i.e. health managers), which will equip them with digital skills needed to exchange information more efficiently and effectively with patients and other professionals.

**Objectives**: Managing the culture change needed to drive learning across health care organisations. The clinical and non-clinical professionals increasingly need to combine their understanding of clinical practice with that of technology and change management to ensure the digital technology fits into the realities of health care practice, to secure the buy-in from the frontline health workers, as well as to manage the culture change needed to drive learning across health care organisations.

**Results**: Enabled and facilitated professionals and non-clinical staff to adopt new digital tools and integrate them into their everyday practices enabling a smoother digital transition.

## WLF: Work–Life Flow

**Funding Agency:** ERASMUS+, National Agency Spain

**Active project years:** 2020–2023

**Active link:** https://www.work-life-flow.eu/

**Membership of Consortium by country:** Spain (co-ordinator), Germany, Ireland, Kosovo, Portugal.

**Aim:** WLF aims at fostering a positive Work–Life Flow (WLF) in post-Corona legacy arising from remote working and social distancing. WLF refers to the dynamic equilibrium between an individual's professional and social roles. The EU-Directive 2019/1158 (European Parliament and of the Council of 20 June 2019) on work–life balance and their concretisation at national levels and the aim of the International Labour Organisation for "Decent Work" show relevance of WLF.

**Objectives:** Mastering a healthy WLF is a challenging key competence to maintain an effective work performance while increasing social, physical and mental health, including working parents and informal carers. A needs analysis of reports (Joint Research Council of EC) and trends in European policy on key competences and work–life balance discovered a skills gap.

Such non-cognitive skills are underdeveloped across the EU's education systems but expected to grow in importance. Therefore, the projects' competency-based approach to WLF is key to foster individual well-being within current and future workforce. The WLF envisioned competences represent one of the eight key competences of life-long learning ("Personal, social and learning to learn") identified by the Council of the European Union.

Results:

- A self-assessment tool identifying the personal situation regarding Decent Work, Work–Life Balance and Well-Being-at-Work, with a link to tutorials offering skills to address identified gaps.
- A self-learning portal to deliver these trainings modules.
- A field-test of the developed tools and tutorials in the consortium regions.
- A book presenting the summarised results to be published by Springer in 2025.

# Appendix C: Free Resources to Help You Write an Application and Manage Your Project

Below you find a short description of tools that we either developed ourselves or adapted from EU provided templates and found helpful for either preparing an EU research application or managing an EU-funded project,

You can download these tools from: http://www.ibk.eu/en/coaching.php

## Project Card

The "Project Card" allows to develop a short introduction on your project idea, it covers the following points

- Existing partners
- Call Reference
- Project idea
- Background
- & Approach
- Project Objectives
- Expected Outcome
- Work Packages
- Innovation
- Impact
- Benefits
- Main products
- Dissemination
- Project Duration
- Deadline for the application
- Expected Funding
- Author/reviser



C.-A. Dalluege, J. S. G. Wells (eds.), *Navigating an EU Research Project*, Management for Professionals, https://doi.org/10.1007/978-3-031-70928-9

The idea is to always have only very short sentences for each bullet point and the whole PC ideally covers just 2 pages A4.

During the proposal writing phase, the PC could be used to address additional partners to join the consortium or win interested parties to sign a Letter of Intent to cooperate with the proposed project as pilot user once the solution has been developed.

Once the project has been funded, the PC can easily be adjusted to serve an initial dissemination paper.

### Resource Matrix Template

A set of interlinked XLS-based tables that allow you to plan you labour resources in detail, calculate your costs and develop the Project GANTT.

With some small changes, as described in Chap. 5, each partner can transform the labour planning table to map their own resource spending against the original task allocation. This will facilitate the financial reporting to the programme office.

### Potential Risks Table

The Potential Risks Table will be asked for in most application forms to evaluate how the consortium is prepared to consider and address future challenges to the project's performance. Our template table already offers some "standard" risks and answer on how to react on them, such as loss of productivity due to communication breaks or lack of pilot user cooperation due to their status of not being bound by a contract to the funding programme.

### Dissemination Table

Our Dissemination Table is based on tables requested by some of the current programmes and gives a few examples of what can be reported and how.

### Business Matrix Canvas: Example for HEI

Many programmes expect the project to develop a post-project dissemination and exploitation plan. This is especially hard for non-profit organisation or pure research institutions, since they normally do not develop any business plans.

Our template gives an example of how Business Matrix Canvas could look like for a university.

# Bibliography


Barbayannis, G., Bandari, M., Zheng, X., Baquerizo, H., Pecor, K. W., & Ming, X. (2022). Academic stress and mental well-being in college students: Correlations, affected groups, and COVID-19. *Frontiers in Psychology, 13*, 886344. https://doi.org/10.3389/fpsyg.2022.886344

Berger, R., Dalluege, C.-A., & Franz, H. W. (2022). *Organisational excellence and resilience: Stress management as a component of a sustainable corporate development strategy*. Springer Nature Switzerland AG.

Caron, F. (2014). Project planning and control: Early engagement of project stakeholders. *The Journal of Modern Project Management, 2*(1).

CORDIS EU research results. Available at: https://cordis.europa.eu/

Dalluege, C.-A. (2012). Mit individuellen Messgrößen zum Erfolg. *Softwarekompendium*, Seite 14-19.

Dalluege, C.-A. Wirtschaft im Wandel – Strategieentwicklung als Konkrete Aufgabe, Controller-Magazin 11/2011, Seite 9-17.

European Commission. Before you apply: EU funding for beginners. Available at: https://commission.europa.eu/funding-tenders/how-apply/you-apply-eu-funding-beginners_en

European Research Executive Agency. Common mistakes to avoid when applying for Horizon Europe funding. Available at: https://rea.ec.europa.eu/news/common-mistakes-avoid-when-applying-horizon-europe-funding-2023-02-09_en

Jessop, D. S. (2019). The power of positive stress and a research roadmap. *Stress, 22*(5), 521–523. https://doi.org/10.1080/10253890.2019.1593365

Martinelli, R. J., & Milosevic, D. Z. (2016). *Project management ToolBox, tools and techniques for the practicing project manage* (2nd ed.). Wiley.

Polit, D. F., & Beck, C. T. (2021). *Nursing research: Generating and assessing evidence for nursing practice* (11th ed.). Wolters Kluwer.

Rowe, S. F. & Sikes, S. (2006). Lessons learned: Taking it to the next level. Paper presented at PMI® Global Congress 2006—North America, Seattle, WA. Newtown Square, PA: Project Management Institute.

Sousa, V. D., & Rojjanasrirat, W. (2011). Translation, adaptation and validation of instruments or scales for use in cross-cultural health care research: A clear and user-friendly guideline. *Journal of Evaluation in Clinical Practice, 17*(2), 268–274. https://doi.org/10.1111/J.1365-2753.2010.01434.X

Ståhl, C. M. (2023). Stress at work: Countering Europe's new pandemic. *Social Europe*. Retrieved 16.53 May 05, 2024 from https://www.socialeurope.eu/stress-at-work-countering-europes-new-pandemic





C.-A. Dalluege, J. S. G. Wells (eds.), *Navigating an EU Research Project*, Management for Professionals, https://doi.org/10.1007/978-3-031-70928-9

Webinar: How to prepare a successful proposal in Horizon Europe. Available at: https://ec.europa.eu/research/participants/docs/h2020-funding-guide/other/event210324.htm

What is a RACI Matrix?. Available at: https://project-management.com/understanding-responsibility-assignment-matrix-raci-matrix/

Yarmolyuk-Kröck, K. (2022) A case for an EU directive addressing work-related psychological risks - An eastern European perspective. In *ETUI*. The European Trade Union Institute. Retrieved 16:41, May 05, 2024, from https://www.etui.org/publications/case-eu-directive-addressing-work-related-psychological-risks

MIX
Papier aus verantwortungsvollen Quellen
Paper from responsible sources
FSC® C105338

If you have any concerns about our products,
you can contact us on
**ProductSafety@springernature.com**

In case Publisher is established outside the EU,
the EU authorized representative is:
**Springer Nature Customer Service Center GmbH**
**Europaplatz 3, 69115 Heidelberg, Germany**

Printed by Libri Plureos GmbH
in Hamburg, Germany